Two on an Island

by BIANCA BRADBURY

Illustrated by Mort Künstler

SCHOLASTIC BOOK SERVICES

NEW YORK • TORONTO • LONDON • AUCKLAND • SYDNEY

Copyright © 1965 by Bianca R. Bradbury. This edition is published by Scholastic Book Services, a division of Scholastic Magazines, Inc., by arrangement with Houghton Mifflin Company.

1st printing . . . . September 1968

Printed in the U.S.A.

Two on an Island

1

JEFF WATCHED THE LITTLE ROWBOAT floating away and kicked his heel in the wet sand angrily. His sister Trudy turned around and laughed in his face. "What's so funny?" Jeff demanded.

She stopped smiling. "I don't know, but there's nothing to get mad about. It just looks kind of gay, that's all."

He saw what she meant. Now that the blue boat had no passengers to weigh it down, it moved as lightly as a sea bird.

"Aren't you going after it?" Trudy asked.

"Of course I'm going after it." Jeff unlaced his sneakers and took off his dungarees and shirt. Stripped to his swimming trunks, he splashed into the water and dove under.

Ever since school closed he had been looking forward to visiting his grandmother, to this first dive into the cold salt harbor. He came up, shook the brown hair out of his eyes. The shock of the cold water was a pure joy. He had been angry with Trudy for not beaching the boat, but he was over it now.

He swam face down, not wasting a motion, glad to find he hadn't forgotten his crawl stroke since last summer. When he came up to breathe he saw that the boat was still a hundred yards away and seemed to be moving faster. He looked back at the shore to measure how far he had come.

Trudy was up to her knees in the water, hanging on to Sarge's leash. The German shepherd was barking wildly and lunging. "Hang onto him," Jeff called. Just then Sarge broke loose from Trudy's grasp.

It didn't matter, for Sarge was a good swimmer. "He'll probably want to race me to the boat," Jeff thought, and swam faster. He glanced back when he came up for air. Sarge was gaining on him, cutting a V through the calm water. Jeff watched him. He and Sarge were more like brothers than like dog and master, and he thought, "This is old Sarge's first swim too, and he's really loving it."

"All right, boy," he called, "let's see who gets there first."

Sarge wasn't aiming for the boat, though. He

reached his master, put his heavy paw on Jeff's back, and pushed him under.

Jeff came up sputtering. "Hey, what's the big idea?"

Sarge seized Jeff's arm in his teeth, not too gently. The dog had missed the whole point of the race, that they were supposed to be catching the boat. His eyes looked worried. "Let go," Jeff ordered.

Sarge's teeth pressed down hard and he yanked Jeff around. It wasn't a game now. The dog meant to drag him back to shore. "Good dog, it's all right. Let go," Jeff told him.

They struggled silently, and half the time Jeff was underwater, trying to break free. He was big-boned, and tall for his twelve years, but he still was no match for a dog Sarge's size. Once he came up and heard Trudy shrieking with fright, "Let him go, Sarge, let him go!" It must have looked to her as though the dog was trying to drown him.

Jeff stopped fighting and turned back to shore. Immediately Sarge released his arm. "You fool!" Jeff yelled at him, but Sarge only watched him, swimming alongside. Jeff swung around once to look for the boat. The tide had caught it and was carrying it beyond the Point.

The dog wasn't even winded when they reached

7

shore. He shook himself and danced around. Jeff lay face down on the hot sand, trying to get his wind back. Finally he let out a big sigh and sat up.

Trudy stood over him, her small face full of trouble. "Why didn't you hang on to that fool of a dog?" Jeff snapped at her.

"Why do you always blame me for everything?" Trudy's big blue eyes filled with tears.

"Because you never do anything right," Jeff said from force of habit.

She turned away and started off, and he called after her. "Don't blubber. We'll go exploring."

Actually, they knew every inch of Middle Hump, knew every blade of grass and stick and stone on it. The Pennells lived fifty miles away in New Millbrook, an inland town, and all year long Jeff and his sister looked forward to visiting their grandmother. Her house was set on a bluff overlooking Bridgeton Harbor.

The harbor was wide, but so shallow that only fishing boats could use it. The city of Bridgeton lay at the head of it, and from Middle Hump Jeff and Trudy could see smoke rising from factory chimneys, and the sparkles where the sun flashed from windows of tall buildings. A new turnpike, built over the salt marshes, edged the city. On a clear day like this they could make out cars rushing along at sixty miles an hour.

Their little island, though, seemed a hundred miles away from the noise of the city and rush of traffic. Once Middle Hump had been part of a bar that almost closed the harbor's mouth. A hurricane had broken the sandbar into three islands. A duck hunter's shack, built on the highest rise, was Middle Hump's only landmark.

They reached the end of their island. One hundred yards away lay East Hump, and beyond that the channel. They tramped back along the other side that faced the Sound. Today the surf was light. The tide had cast up some interesting things, but Jeff didn't stop to examine them. They walked on to the western point. Here two hundred yards of water separated the island from West Hump.

They had circled their private island. Now Trudy said, "I'm hungry."

"Who isn't?" Jeff said. "We had breakfast at six, and it must be two o'clock. It's lucky we swiped some food at Gram's."

They broke into a run. Luckily they had unloaded the rowboat when they first arrived. Their bags of cookies and bananas and the Thermos of milk were safely tucked under Jeff's jacket at the edge of the beach grass.

Sarge stood over it, guarding it. Jeff pulled him away. "You're a pretty good old dog after all," he said. "You could have eaten our lunch while we were gone."

"I'm glad we've got an honest dog," Trudy said happily. "Just for that you get a whole cookie, dog."

She reached in the bag, but Jeff grabbed it away none too gently. "Hey, don't be a pig!" Trudy yelled.

For once Jeff didn't yell back. "I'm not being a pig," he said. "I just think we ought to go easy on the food. We ought to ration it."

"Why?"

For the past hour, while they strolled around the island, a small worry had been working around in Jeff's mind. Now he said reluctantly, "Our boat's gone, remember? So we don't know how long we'll be here. We've got to make the food last."

He gave Sarge a piece of oatmeal cookie. The big dog wolfed it down in a single bite and wagged his tail, begging for more. Trudy sat holding hers, looking solemn. Then she said, "That's silly. Gram will send somebody to get us."

"Will she?" Then Jeff added, "Well, maybe she will."

He divided a banana. Trudy took her share, then ate her cookie in about four bites, and the dog dove for the crumbs she dropped. She drank the half cup of milk Jeff measured out for her. Sarge got no milk, although he asked for it.

Trudy scrambled up. "I'm going to pick up shells until somebody comes."

"You do that," Jeff said. He really wanted to be left alone.

He buried the Thermos bottle at the edge of the

marsh grass, where the sand was cooler than in the hot sun. He counted the cookies. There were seven left. The other bag held four bananas. He carefully wrapped the bags in his jacket, hid it in the grass, and laid a dry board over it. Then he sat clasping his knees, staring across the water toward the city, trying to straighten out his thoughts.

He went back over what had happened. This was Tuesday. Gram wasn't expecting him and his sister until Friday. The plans had been made for a long time. Mr. and Mrs. Pennell were going to drive the children to Gram's house, stay overnight, and go home the next morning.

This plan had been changed on Monday evening. "Was that only last night?" Jeff thought. The Bensons, who lived next door, had come for supper. While they were eating, Mrs. Benson happened to mention that she and her husband were leaving for their vacation the next day. "Trudy and Jeff are going away too," Mrs. Pennell said. "We're driving them to Bridgeton Friday."

"Why don't you let us take them? We go right through there," Mr. Benson suggested.

"That's a lovely idea," Mrs. Pennell told him. "We'll call my husband's mother and make sure it's all right for them to come a few days early."

Trudy spoke up. "No — let us surprise her," she begged. "Gram's always home anyway, and it would be fun just to pop in on her."

It was settled that way, and after the Bensons went home Jeff and Trudy packed their bags and went to bed early, to be ready for a six o'clock start.

But Gram hadn't been home. When Mr. Benson drove up in front of her house and Trudy jumped out to bang on the door, Gram hadn't answered. They sat in the car, trying to decide what to do.

Sarge was tired of being cooped up, and whined to get out. Jeff handed Trudy his leash and ordered her to hold him. Jeff went around to the back to get their suitcases out of the luggage compartment.

Just then a white cat darted out of Gram's bushes. Sarge gave a mighty heave and threw off his collar and tore off down the street after the cat. Jeff shouted at him, but Sarge was really gone.

"You'd better not wait, sir," he told Mr. Benson. "Gram will be home soon. We don't want to hold you up."

"Are you sure you children will be all right?" Mrs. Benson leaned out to ask.

"We'll be fine. Thanks for the ride. Good-bye!"

Jeff was anxious to start looking for Sarge. The Bensons drove away.

He was still holding the two bags. He didn't want anyone to steal them, so he tossed them into the clump of bushes at the corner of Gram's yard. Then he set off after Sarge.

He had a long, hot run before he cornered the police dog several blocks away. He slipped Sarge's collar on and yanked him back to Gram's.

By this time all Jeff could think of was a cool swim. When they dressed that morning, both he and Trudy had put on their swimsuits under their clothes, so they wouldn't have to waste time changing after they reached Gram's.

Trudy had found the back door unlocked. She and Jeff rummaged in the kitchen for food. They swiped bananas and cookies and filled a Thermos bottle with milk. Trudy thought they ought to leave Gram a note, but Jeff was still hot and angry from chasing Sarge. "Come on if you're coming," he ordered. "The tide's high now, so we can't waste time. Gram will know we're here when she finds the food gone. We'll be back in a couple of hours."

He took the oars and oarlocks from the garage and they crossed the street and followed the cinder path down the bluff, across the salt marsh to the dock. Several other boats were tied there. Trudy gave a cry of delight when she saw theirs, for it was freshly painted a bright blue. They stowed their lunch aboard, Sarge scrambled in, and Jeff rowed out to Middle Hump.

So here they were. But now they were boatless.

Jeff was still sitting in the same spot when his sister came back from shell collecting. Her prize was a quahog shell as big as a saucer. She wanted him to see it, but Jeff didn't look, and she held it in front of his face. Jeff pushed her arm away.

Trudy had a spitfire temper of her own. "What makes you so mean?" she demanded. "Why can't you be nice, like other people?"

"Other people don't have a pest like you for a sister!" Jeff snarled back. "And what's nice about the fix we're in? Answer me that!"

"What fix?" Trudy said. "Somebody will come soon."

"That's what *you* think!"

She grabbed a handful of sand, ready to throw it at him. Then she stopped. The worry that had been nagging Jeff must have shown in his face. Trudy said uncertainly, "Somebody will come."

"Maybe so, maybe not," Jeff told her. "You'd better get used to the idea, pest. You and I are marooned."

15

2

J EFF HAD NEVER STOPPED TO WONDER whether he really liked this nine-year-old sister of his or not. As long as he could remember, Trudy had been a pest, tagging after him, getting in his way.

Gram laid down only one law, when they visited her: "You can stay if you don't fight. But the first angry word I hear from either of you, back you go to your own folks, fast!" It always put a terrible strain on them to be nice to each other for two whole weeks.

So now Jeff was pleased to see that his sister was beginning to worry. "What time is it?" she asked.

He gauged the height of the sun in the sky. "It's after four o'clock, I guess."

"Gram must be home by now," Trudy said. "She wouldn't leave the back door unlocked if she was going to be away very long. Isn't that right?"

"I suppose so."

16

"She's come home by now and found our suit-cases and guessed we came over here. So she's probably asked one of the neighbors who owns a boat to look for us."

Jeff was silent, staring across toward the city. "Isn't that the way it is?" Trudy insisted.

"Maybe." Jeff got to his feet.

"Where are you going?"

"Nowhere."

"I'm not coming with you," Trudy said. "I'm going to watch for the boat."

Sarge had been dozing with his long nose on his paws. When Jeff glanced back he saw him follow-ing, carefully stepping in his master's footprints. Sandpipers winged up, but Sarge didn't bother to chase them. Jeff saw that he too sensed that some-thing was wrong.

The tide was past the full now. That was what had fooled Jeff about the boat. When they first reached the island the tide had seemed high, and he hadn't bothered to pull the boat up beyond its reach. He had unloaded it and then run across the island to see how the surf was on the Sound side. Trudy had been playing at the water's edge near the boat. She hadn't noticed when the tide gently lifted it and carried it off. That was why Jeff had a good excuse for blaming her.

The harbor was so shallow that the water went out fast. Soon mud flats would edge the shore. Jeff knew all too well that nobody could get a boat in or out except at high tide. Most of the time the mud flats made the dock useless. Unless Gram had already sent somebody to look for them, that person would have to wait for the next high tide.

It must have been high around three o'clock. It wouldn't be high again until after three the next morning.

When he reached the southern tip, Jeff saw how fast the water was receding. At low tide the water that separated Middle Hump from West Hump would shrink to a narrow channel. If it was sandy, Jeff could walk it. He could cross West Hump, wade through the salt marshes, and reach the shore of West Bridgeton, where Gram lived.

The trouble was that Bridgeton Harbor had what fishermen and sailors called the worst mud in the world. They said that when you walked into it as far as your knees, you couldn't move. It stank and it was like glue.

Jeff strolled slowly back, his arms folded over his stomach. One cookie since breakfast wasn't much.

Trudy watched him come. "The tide's going out fast," she said. "If Gram asked the Ryan boys or

18

Mr. Schultz to row out to get us, they ought to be here by now."

Jeff made no answer.

"What time will the tide be high again?"

"Sometime after three."

"Three tomorrow morning?"

"That's right."

Her big brown eyes filled with tears and she let out a sob. "Oh, Jeff!"

"Look, this isn't the worst thing in the world that could happen to us," he said rapidly. "What if we do have to stay here tonight, what's so horrible about that? It's warm, and we've got food. And think of the story we'll have to tell!"

"Dad and Mother won't like it."

"That's a silly thing to say, because they're home and we're here, and it's happened and there's nothing anybody can do about it. We're marooned, kid. Let's see what we can do to get ready, in case we have to spend the night. Then if somebody comes it's okay, and if we stay that'll be okay too."

Trudy's eyes cleared. Jeff was looking at her, really seeing her, and the strangest thought crossed his mind. His sister wasn't a bad-looking kid. The way she did her long light-brown hair in two Indian braids was kind of cute. She was slim and tanned, and even in dungarees and an old red blouse she looked better than most kids.

If anybody had asked him yesterday what his sister was like, he would have snorted, "She's nothing but a little creep." Now he thought, "She doesn't look so creepy."

This was a weird way to be thinking about somebody you'd been fighting with all your life, who was always getting in your hair and getting you in wrong with your parents and everybody else.

When she spoke he expected her to say something disagreeable. Instead she asked, "What'll we do to get ready?" She was actually asking his advice. This was really something new.

"Let's break into the shack," Jeff suggested. "We've always wanted to, and now we've got a good excuse."

They pushed through stiff beach grass to reach it. It faced the Sound, its weathered door closed with a rusted padlock. It measured about ten feet each way. One of the three windows had been broken as long as Jeff could remember, but the glass in the other two was intact.

"Doesn't it look about the same as it did last year?" Trudy asked.

Every summer they had talked about going inside it to explore. Gram had ordered, "Don't you touch it. It belongs to whoever built it. You'd be trespassing."

"It's a little more beat up," Jeff said. "Look, though. The lock's just about ready to fall off."

The hasp which held the padlock hung by only one rusty nail. Jeff grasped it and twisted, and it came off in his hand.

"Gram said it would be trespassing to go inside," Trudy warned him.

"Gram didn't have it in mind that we might be marooned over here," Jeff said grimly.

The door sagged, and with a shriek of old iron the hinges let go. Jeff propped it aside and they peered in. "Hey, it's nice," Trudy whispered.

The hut had been abandoned for years, and yet it was in good condition. A bunk made of boards took up one side. A rickety table stood under the broken window, an upended orange crate in the corner. A shelf across the back still held a pile of newspapers and cans and boxes. The sagging mattress and folded blankets on the bunk gave off a musty smell.

Trudy pulled Jeff back. "There might be snakes!"

"There aren't any snakes on Middle Hump, dopey. You stay here until I drag the stuff out so we can air it."

He held his breath and picked up the mattress and threw it out the door, and the blankets after it. Trudy spread them open to catch the sun. "I don't see why other kids haven't wrecked the shack," she said.

"Not many people come out here," Jeff reminded her. "Last summer we saw some clam diggers, but that's the only time I can remember. We usually have the island to ourselves."

Trudy shivered when she stepped inside. The air did feel sticky. Jeff was wrestling with a window when a floorboard let go under his feet with a loud crack. The floor was rotten, and the whole shack was just about ready to collapse. It was a wonder the wind hadn't blown it down long before. Jeff shook the wooden bunk to see if that was going to collapse too, but it seemed fairly steady.

"It's only wide enough for one," Trudy noted.

"You're a girl, so that means you get it," Jeff said. "I never could figure out why girls always get the best of every deal."

Trudy didn't seem to want to fight. She wandered outside. A fishing boat was coming in, lying low in the water. It was a quarter mile away, too far for anyone on board to hear a shout. When it followed the channel around the end of East Hump, it would come closer to the shore.

Trudy was hugging her stomach too, but she didn't mention that she was hungry. She said with a funny little smile, "I guess a Girl Scout ought to know what to do in a fix like this, but I don't."

"I always told you that Scouting was silly stuff," Jeff said.

She didn't rise to this bait either. Trudy had belonged to a Brownie troop and loved it, and now she was thrilled to be a Junior Girl Scout. Her Scout friends were always hanging around the house. Jeff had joined the Boy Scouts, but had gone to only a few meetings and then stopped. The boys in the troop didn't seem to like him.

He couldn't admit the truth. Trudy had scores of friends; she always had a gang to play with. Jeff was sort of a lone wolf, and prided himself on it. What did he care if he didn't get along with other boys?

Trudy was scuffing sand with her sneaker. She called, "I'm going across the island to see if anybody's coming."

Jeff was relieved to be left alone. He thought to himself, "If I didn't have a dumb girl along, this being marooned would be fun."

He couldn't think of anything else to do. The blankets and mattress ought to be left out to air as long as there was sun to dry them. Sarge was barking at the far end of the island, and Jeff strolled that way.

The dog had found a horseshoe crab and was playing with it. It was trying to get back to the water, but Sarge circled it, dashing at it and jumping away when it moved. The huge crab was safe inside its solid shell and seemed to know it, and kept edging toward the water.

Jeff picked it up by its horny tail and flipped it over on its back. Its legs waved helplessly in the air. Sarge lunged closer.

Trudy had come up, hearing the racket. "That was a mean thing to do," she said, and with her toe turned the crab right side up.

Jeff promptly flipped it over on its back again.

Suddenly his sister was furiously angry. She struck out at him. Then she seized the crab by its tail and flung it far out to shallow water. It scuttled safely away.

Jeff pinned his sister's arms to her sides. "What do you mean, interfering with Sarge's game?"

"He's a dog, and he doesn't know better, but you ought to," she sputtered.

"What does one old crab matter?"

"It matters a lot to a crab," she said, and jerked away from him and ran off.

Who was he angry with, Trudy or the stupid

horseshoe crab or himself? Jeff didn't know. He stalked on, rounded the point, and came to the place where the food was hidden in the tall grass. He sat down and glowered across the water.

The sun was low now in the western sky. Jeff guessed it must be about seven o'clock. Traffic flowed along the turnpike; he saw the flashes as the windshields caught the late sun.

He was still annoyed with Trudy. Who did she think she was, telling him what was right and wrong? It would serve her right if he ate all the food.

His mouth was dry, and the thought of a moist, sweet banana made him even thirstier. He opened the bag, broke one off, and was just about to peel it and eat it all.

Something stopped him. When he came right down to it, he couldn't eat the banana alone and in secret. He gathered up the bags and his jacket and marched across the island to the shack.

Trudy sat in the doorway with Sarge sprawled beside her, his head in her lap. She smiled timidly, as though she was hoping Jeff wasn't cross. Sarge sat up expectantly at sight of the bags. "We might as well eat," Jeff said.

Trudy didn't argue with the way he divided the food. She took the cookie and the half of a banana he carefully cut with a clean shell. "Eat slowly," he advised. "It fills you up better that way."

That advice was wasted on Sarge. He swallowed his piece of cookie in one bite and eyed the Thermos hopefully.

He got no milk. Trudy said, troubled, "He must be awfully thirsty." But Jeff wouldn't yield on that point.

"He can have my share," Trudy insisted.

"Don't be a fool," Jeff said harshly. "A swallow of milk wouldn't do him much good, and you need it worse."

"But when people come to find us tomorrow morning we'll still have food left!"

"We'll worry about that when the time comes."

When their meal was over they aimlessly wan-

dered over to the harbor side and sat there through the dusk, until dark. Over there in the city, thousands of people were eating dinner. Afterward they would look at television for a while and then they would go to bed. Nobody over there knew that two children were marooned on the empty island at the mouth of the harbor.

Jeff felt such an awful loneliness it was like pain, and he could hardly stand it. Out of all those thousands of people, nobody cared what happened to him and his sister.

27

Not even Gram? What was the matter with Gram? She ought to have called the police by now. Somebody ought to have come.

Trudy moved closer. The stars blazed overhead, and the sand had cooled. There was no use watching any longer, hoping against hope that a boat would appear.

Jeff didn't know how to face up to his loneliness. He was afraid he might start blubbering like a baby, and he hadn't cried since he was five years old. "We'll get ready for bed now. Come on," he ordered.

By starlight they dragged the mattress in and spread one musty blanket over it. Jeff laid his on the floor. They left the door open.

Trudy was doing her best to be brave, and Jeff realized she was holding her breath. "Don't cry," he said. "Please don't cry, Trudy." The gentleness in his tone surprised him.

"If I reach out, can I touch you?"

"Yes, I'm right here."

"Jeff, why didn't somebody come?"

"I don't know. I really don't," he said.

"Somebody will come in the morning."

"Yes," Jeff said, "somebody will come in the morning."

3

TRUDY REACHED OVER AND TOUCHED HIM, to make sure he was near. Then she curled up, and soon her even breathing told Jeff she was asleep.

He stared out the door, not even seeing the far-away stars. What he hadn't mentioned to his sister made him tremble uncontrollably now.

He wasn't at all sure they would be rescued in the morning. It had occurred to him that Gram might not find the suitcases.

He went over in his mind exactly what had happened: Mr. Benson had parked the car in front of Gram's house. Trudy had been holding Sarge's leash while Jeff opened the luggage compartment to take out the suitcases. Sarge had slipped out of his collar and taken off after the white cat. Mrs. Benson had said that she and her husband ought to wait, to make sure Gram came home all right. Jeff had told her, "No, we'll be all right."

What had happened next? He had set the bags on the curb and waved good-bye to the Bensons. As soon as the car drove off he had tossed the bags into the shrubbery, so that nobody could steal them while he chased the dog.

He had captured Sarge, and after that he had been so hot and eager to get out on the water he had forgotten all about the suitcases.

Those syringa and rhododendron bushes at the corner of Gram's yard made a wonderful secret place. He and Trudy often used them when they wanted to hide. They were thick and high, and anything you threw in there just disappeared.

Jeff was trying to think the thing through logically. If Gram didn't find the bags, how else could she guess they had been in the house? She might not miss the cookies. Would she notice, though, that a bottle of milk was gone? Jeff remembered putting the empty carton in the wastepaper basket under the sink. When Gram opened the refrigerator, would she see that some bananas had been broken off the big bunch? And how about the Thermos bottle — would she miss it?

Jeff was very fond of his father's mother, and

one thing he liked about her was that she wasn't too fussy a housekeeper, like some women. Her house was big and comfortable, but not even her best friend would claim it was tidy. Leaving the kitchen door unlocked was just like Gram. She was careless about things like that. She kept her pantry and her refrigerator stuffed with food, and she wasn't the type to count cookies or bananas.

"While we were swiping stuff, I wish we'd swiped enough so she'd have to notice," he thought.

Then he suddenly stopped thinking and froze. Not two feet away from his head an animal began gnawing. It wasn't Sarge, who lay against Jeff's legs, sleeping.

The bag of food was on the table. Jeff heard paper tear, and the faint dry rustle of feet. Sarge's heavy breathing stopped, and Jeff felt him stiffen. Sarge growled deep in his throat.

Trudy started up. "What's the matter? What's the matter?"

"It's rats! They're after the food!"

As he yelled, Jeff reached out to snatch the precious bag of food. A heavy body, then another fell off the table and landed on him, then shot out the door. Sarge rushed after, snarling and barking.

Trudy screamed wildly. The word "rat" had set

31

her off. Jeff shuddered, remembering the heavy
bodies running across him. But he got hold of himself. "It's all right," he said harshly. "Stop that
noise! We'll take our blankets outside."

She still blubbered, but followed him. He spread
the blanket on the beach and ordered "Lie down,"
and she did as she was told.

Sarge came back from his useless chase and flung
himself down between them on the blanket. He
nosed at the bag of food Jeff clutched in his arms,
but didn't beg. His size and warmth were a comfort.

By the faint light Jeff saw that tears were silently
slipping down Trudy's face. "I'm scared to go to
sleep again," she whispered.

"It'll be all right. They won't bother us out here."

"How many were there?"

"Only two."

"Were they big?"

"They felt about the size of cats when they landed on me."

"Jeff, I'm thirsty," she said. "I'm terribly thirsty."

"So'm I. Go to sleep."

"We could have one little sip of milk."

"No, we can't."

Trudy said angrily, "Just because you're bigger you think you're the boss. You're a pig, that's what you are. It's no wonder nobody likes you."

"Why don't you shut up?" Jeff said coldly.

She was silent for a while, hugging Sarge's big head against her. Then she said in a small voice, "I'm sorry, I didn't mean it about being a pig and nobody liking you. That's not true."

"I don't care whether you meant it or whether it's true or not. You don't get any milk until morning."

She said no more. Jeff stared up at the stars swimming in the infinite sky. For the first time in their lives Trudy had put into words what Jeff had been suspecting for a long time. There was something about him that made it hard for people to like him. Oh, his parents did. Maybe, though, it was their duty to love him because he was their son.

Jeff knew he was too stiff with people when they

wanted to be friendly. He couldn't help it, for he didn't know how to change. Here he and Trudy were, in probably the worst trouble of their lives. He wanted to comfort her and be nice, but he just couldn't. He didn't know how. The habit of scolding and bossing was too strong.

Everywhere else in the world people were safe in their beds. Jeff and Trudy were utterly alone on their tiny island in the night. They ought to be together in their trouble, but they weren't. They were as far apart as though miles lay between them.

Trudy gave a sigh that ended in a sob, turned over, and pressed against the warm body of the dog and slept. Jeff dozed too.

When he awoke, the eastern sky was pink. Clouds were breaking, the clear sky showing through. His sister and Sarge were gone.

He found Trudy on the other side of the island scanning the harbor. Fishing boats were putting out from Oyster Point, but there were no small boats in sight.

She had forgotten their quarrel in the night and turned to him. "What time was the tide high this morning, Jeff?"

"Two or three hours ago, I guess. It'll be full at four this afternoon. It's an hour later every day, you know," Jeff reminded her.

"It was dark then, but just the same you'd think somebody would have come out looking for us."

Jeff said nothing.

Trudy went on. "Gram must have told the police by now. Don't the police have boats, so they can rescue people?"

"I suppose so," Jeff said.

Trudy's small face looked pinched and unhappy. "I don't understand it. I should think everybody would be out looking for us. Even if Gram didn't tell the police, she'd at least tell the neighbors."

Jeff hesitated, and she insisted. "Isn't that so?"

"I suppose so."

"The tide's going out now, so they can't get away from that stupid dock. We're going to have to wait until this afternoon. Jeff, what's the matter with Gram and everybody? Don't they care?"

She might as well know, Jeff thought, and said just that. "You might as well know, kid. Gram might not find out until Friday that we're lost."

"What do you mean?"

"We weren't due to get here until Friday. Don't forget, you were the one who had the bright idea we ought to surprise Gram. Nobody called her to let her know the Bensons were bringing us, so she didn't expect us yesterday."

35

"You're just trying to scare me," Trudy said. "How does she think our suitcases got there? Does she think they flew all by themselves?"

"Try to remember what happened," Jeff told her. "Sarge took off, and before I chased him I threw the bags in the bushes. Who's going to prowl around in those bushes and find them? You'd better forget about them and start hoping Gram notices that some of her food is missing."

"Okay," Trudy said doubtfully, "I'll start hoping that."

"You do that little thing," Jeff said.

Trudy knew the worst now. She was just a girl, and Jeff thought, "Trust girls, they always go to pieces when they get scared."

The thought crossed his mind that he himself had never had a chance to prove whether he was brave or not. He let that pass. Boys didn't go to pieces, so he didn't have to worry whether he would behave all right.

He watched Trudy, expecting her to burst into tears. She didn't; she just said, "Let's eat now."

He felt like asking her, "Can't you think of anything but your confounded stomach?" but he didn't. If hers felt as tight and empty as his did, it was no wonder she kept thinking about it.

They opened the precious bags of food. Sarge

noticed, but this time he didn't come frisking and barking. He slunk over with his tail between his legs.

Jeff divided one banana, then carefully broke a cookie and gave Trudy half. "Let's have our milk too," she suggested. "These cookies are kind of dry. How about Sarge?"

"We need the food worse than he does," Jeff said.

"No, we don't. He's just a dumb beast, so he doesn't know what's the matter. He acts starved."

"Humans are more important."

Trudy's jaw set stubbornly. "I don't believe that's so. I'll give him mine."

Jeff scowled. "Go ahead. Then it'll be your tough luck if you go hungry all day."

Trudy broke her half cookie into quarters. "Here, boy," she called. Sarge swallowed his piece in one bite. Trudy marched away down the beach, and her stiff back showed her scorn for her brother.

Jeff was angry with her, and with himself too. He ought to let her go, to teach her who was boss, to show he didn't care about her grandstand play, giving her food away to the dog. But he didn't. He shouted after her, "Come on back, I was only kidding."

She walked slowly back, and he handed her a

share of his own cookie. He opened the Thermos of milk and carefully filled the small cup for her. Trudy's face wrinkled. "It's sour!"

"It can't be." Jeff tasted it and almost spat out the milk. "Drink it," he ordered. "Sour milk won't hurt you, and it's better than none. There's not much, so we'll finish it all."

She did as she was told, but tears slipped down her face, and Jeff understood. It seemed like a little thing, the milk going sour. Usually such a small accident wouldn't mean a thing. You just threw the milk away. Today this seemed like a real tragedy. Probably Trudy had been looking forward all night to the taste of cool sweet milk, just as he had.

Something in Jeff's tight, hard heart let go in that moment. He watched Trudy obediently drinking the milk as he had commanded. He would have liked to say something pleasant, but he couldn't think of a thing.

He drank some sour milk himself, then set the cup down for Sarge to finish it. The dog licked out the last drop, then started to chew the plastic cup, and Jeff took it away.

"That was a nice thing to do, Jeff," Trudy said politely. "Now I guess I'll go for a walk."

Jeff had a feeling she wanted to be alone. She often went off by herself when she felt unhappy.

When she was a little girl, she had always run away and hid after they had quarreled. Jeff remembered his mother saying helplessly, "Jeff, what's the matter? Do you want your little sister to hate you?"

Now, stuck on this empty island together, it was still easy to find mean words, hard to find pleasant ones. Jeff let Trudy go and didn't call after her.

He scuffed sand, thinking deeply. Finally he made up his mind. Somehow he was going to get away from this island.

He set out, carrying the bag of food with him, for he didn't trust Sarge any more. The dog was too hungry to be honest. Sarge followed him. They reached the eastern point. The tide was dead low, and a black expanse of stinking mud lay between Middle and East Hump, only a trickle of clean water flowing through the middle.

Jeff had two choices. He could either walk or swim. West Hump was too far, and he could never swim such a distance. He might make East Hump this afternoon when the tide came in. At home he had taught himself to swim the length of the public pool four times without stopping. He could easily manage the few hundred feet to East Hump. Once he got there, he would be farther than ever from the shore and civilization. However, the channel swung in close to East Hump, and a passing boat might be able to take him and Trudy off.

In the meantime he could try walking. "I bet this old mud isn't as bad as they say it is," he thought. He left his sneakers on the shore and stepped in. He gritted his teeth and kept going until the black ooze covered his legs halfway to his knees. He felt the horrible stuff giving under his feet. The mud didn't seem to have any bottom. He got the feeling he would soon sink over his head, and turned and struggled back to shore.

The fishermen were right. Nobody could walk in such mud. If you got in as far as your waist, you wouldn't be able to move your legs. That was the end of that hope; at low tide he would never be able to reach West Hump and safe ground and home.

He looked at his legs and shuddered with disgust, for he had no way to wash them. The mud would have to dry on them until the tide came in.

He rambled back to the shack. Trudy had spread out the blankets in the sun, and they were beginning to smell better. Jeff took the boxes and cans down from the shelf and carried them outside. The box of flour was empty; the rats had finished it long ago. The smaller box, which had held dried beans, was also empty. The cans were so old the labels had fallen off.

There was one large one and two small ones, and although the tops were rusted, the smaller cans seemed tight. Something sloshed inside them. The larger one bulged at the top. Jeff shook it, and rust powdered off, and a smell came out that was so awful Jeff hurled it as far as he could across the mud.

He turned around and saw he had an audience. Trudy had come up. "There's something wet in two of the cans," he told her.

Trudy wasn't listening. She said, "Jeff, what if Mother doesn't happen to call Gram? We could be stuck here until Friday."

"Something will happen before then," Jeff said.

"But it could be Friday."

"Maybe."

"What if Gram waits until Friday night before she telephones Mother and Dad to find out why we didn't come? What about that?"

Jeff was silent, and Trudy said, "Today's only Wednesday."

Jeff said carefully, not growling at her as he usually did, "At the worst we could only be stuck here two more days. We're not stupid, and we're not helpless. But I think we ought to make plans."

4

THEY MOVED INSIDE THE SHACK to escape the noonday sun. The way Trudy was waiting for Jeff to explain gave him a queer feeling. For the first time in her happy-go-lucky life she seemed to be looking up to him, as a younger sister ought to.

He hadn't had any plan of action really, but now he set his thoughts in order. "First we'll look for a can opener," he said. "The men who used this shack left cans here, so they must have used one.

"We'll do that now. Then this afternoon, when the tide's high, I'm going to swim over to East Hump. The fishing boats come in around five or six o'clock. The channel swings in so close, they'll hear me yell.

"There are other things we can do. We'll go beachcombing and collect all the wood that's floated in. We'll look for big shells. Then we'll dig in the middle of the island. There just might be a chance we'll hit fresh water. Probably it's not a very good chance, but it'll give us something to do."

Maybe these suggestions of his weren't too brilliant, but Jeff was amazed to see the effect they had on Trudy. The pinched look of worry left her face, and she laughed happily. "Let's start!" she cried.

"I thought of something too," she went on. "Maybe by now somebody has found our boat. Whoever found it might put an ad in the paper to ask for a reward, and Gram might see it."

"Maybe," Jeff said, "but let's not count on that. There could be a hundred blue boats tied up around this harbor."

"Somebody who lives on Gram's street might see the ad, then, and notice that Gram's boat is missing," Trudy insisted.

"Maybe you're right. Now let's look for a can opener."

They searched the shack and found nothing. "It probably fell through the cracks in the floor," Jeff suggested. Even without tools it was easy for him to rip out the loose, rotting boards. They started turning over the sand underneath, sifting it with their fingers.

It was so steamy hot in the shack Trudy begged to go for a swim, promising to continue the search later, and Jeff agreed.

Her face and arms and legs were turning fiery red, and Jeff realized she was getting a bad burn. His own legs and arms were beginning to hurt. The water was the only place where they could escape the heat.

The beach that faced the Sound had a sandy bottom. The tide was halfway in. They stripped to their swimsuits and ran out. "Don't swallow any water," Jeff warned.

It was clear, green, and cold, and the temptation to wet their mouths with it was very strong. Jeff swam out, but when he saw that Sarge was following he turned back. He was in no condition to fight the big police dog today. Trudy lay at the water's edge, letting the low waves flow over her.

"We'll get burned worse if we stay in the water very long," Jeff fussed. "The sun reflects up from it."

It was queer to think of the sun as an enemy. Usually they hoped only for clear days when they came to visit their grandmother. Now the great red ball blazing in an empty sky was a menace.

If Jeff and Trudy blistered, they would be in

real trouble. Jeff had had that experience. Once he had been caught out on the water by the receding tide, and had waited for hours to get the boat back to the dock. Gram had used all her own remedies, then finally called a doctor, and Jeff had spent several days in bed with a fever. He remembered all too well the fat, agonizing blisters on his shoulders and back.

"Come on," he ordered, "we can't stay out here."

"We can't go back inside the shack," Trudy protested.

Sarge broke up the argument. He buried his face in the water and began to drink. Jeff seized his collar and threw him back on the shore.

Instead of wagging his tail and barking as he always did when he thought Jeff wanted to play, Sarge growled. He broke away, and when Jeff reached for him again he snarled, baring his teeth. "Leave him alone," Trudy pleaded.

"I can't. He'll die if he drinks sea water."

"He'll bite you if you touch him again," Trudy said. "What's the matter with him? Did you ever believe Sarge could act like that?"

"He's thirstier than we realized," Jeff said worriedly.

Sarge went up the beach, put his head in the

water again, and drank. Then he slunk off, walked to the edge of the beach grass, and threw himself down, his nose on his paws, watching them warily.

"Maybe it's not true that sea water will poison you," Trudy said.

"Are you thinking of trying it?"

"I'm so thirsty I could die," Trudy said defiantly. "Look at Sarge. Nothing very awful seems to have happened to him."

"The salt in it will only make you thirstier. Don't you dare try it!"

Trudy didn't answer.

"Did you hear me? Do you promise?"

"Yes I heard you, and yes I promise!" Trudy snapped.

Sarge walked off into the grass and disappeared, and they heard him throwing up. When he came back, he laid down again with his tongue hanging out, looking miserable. Trudy went to him and sat beside him.

Jeff guessed how she felt. Being marooned on a hot, dry island was bad enough. Having their best friend turn against them was more than Trudy could bear. She had to make friends with Sarge, and she was right. Being stuck here with a hostile dog would be dangerous.

Jeff approached him. "Good dog," he said, and put out his hand palm up.

Sarge sniffed it and his tail thumped the sand. Jeff sat on the other side of him, and Sarge laid his rough head on Jeff's knee.

They had been marooned now for exactly twenty-four hours. Jeff and Trudy had shared a quart of milk. Sarge had had only a few drops. How long could a dog live without fluids?

Jeff left his fellow islanders and prowled along the shore. He soon found an unbroken quahog shell six inches long, which would make a good shovel. Trudy called, "What are you going to do?"

"Nothing," he said. There was no point in getting her hopes up, for he probably would find no fresh water.

He chose a high spot on the crown of the island, got down on his knees, and scraped away the sand. He soon came to damp sand. He dug a hole straight down, two feet deep. Water started to seep in, and he sat back on his heels and waited. When the bottom of his hole had an inch of water in it, he tasted.

It was as salty as the ocean itself. They weren't going to get drinkable water that way.

The sun blazed down. The tide was creeping up. As Jeff slowly walked back to his companions, he saw that Trudy was lying in the water again. "What's the use of arguing?" Jeff thought. "Maybe she knows what's best for her."

He took her bandanna out of the pocket of her dungarees and spread it over her face to keep the sun off. She lifted one corner, looked at him with surprise. "Thanks," she said. He sat with her, his legs in the cool water. Sarge joined them, but didn't try again to drink.

The sun and heat and thirst were their enemies, and time was an enemy too. It dragged. The sun had a long, long way to go before it would sink in the western sky.

Jeff was getting so tense he felt as though every nerve in his body was jumping. He wandered down the beach, found a few boards, and dragged them back. He joined Trudy again and scratched lines in the sand, waiting for the incoming tide to creep up to them. Finally he decided the tide was near high and told his sister, "I'm going to swim to East Hump now."

"I'm going with you."

"No — you stay here. You can go back to the shack and try to find something we can open the cans with. And I want you to put on your dungarees."

"I can't! They're so dirty and stiff I'd die in them."

"Put them on," he ordered. "They'll save your legs from burning worse."

Trudy's little face was scarlet and distorted. She was a happy child, and had done so little crying in her life she didn't do it well. She bellowed, "Please, Jeff, I've got to go with you!"

"You can't, Trudy," he said reasonably. "I'll have a tough enough time making East Hump alone."

"What if you get over there and can't get back?"

"I'll get back, don't you worry. Don't let the bag of food out of your sight for a minute. I don't know whether we can trust Sarge, and besides — " Jeff stopped before he mentioned rats.

Trudy read his mind, though. "Where do the rats live?" she asked.

"I don't know. It's funny, because there's no place for them to hide."

"What do they live on?"

"I was thinking about that," Jeff said. "I suppose they eat dead fish that wash up on the shore, if they get to them before the gulls do. But if they're so bold they'd come into the shack the way they did last night, they'd get at the food before

you could stop them, if you forgot and left it somewhere."

Sarge had moved inside the shack, and lay dull-
eyed and panting. Jeff propped the door shut so
the dog couldn't follow him into the water.

Trudy walked to the end of the island with him,
carrying their precious parcel wrapped in Jeff's
shirt. The idea crossed Jeff's mind that after he was
gone there was nothing to stop her from eating all
the remaining cookies and bananas. He decided
not to worry about that. He had been really getting
acquainted with his sister these past two days, and
he had a strong feeling she could be trusted not to
cheat.

They stared at the expanse of water between
them and the eastern island. Now that he faced it,
it looked to Jeff more like a mile than a few hundred yards. "Go on back now," he said. "I'll be all
right."

"I want to go too," she said stubbornly.

"Will you go back as I tell you and put on your
dungarees, or else stay inside the shack out of the
sun?"

She turned obediently.

Jeff waded in and swam with a slow, steady
crawl. Luckily there was no wind. He made the

mistake once of looking up to see how far he had to go. From water-level view the island still seemed a great distance off. Panic seized him, and he breathed hard. The strength ebbed out of his arms and legs, and he began to sink. He turned over on his back and floated, closing his eyes against the sun's glare, resting.

He got his nerve back and resolutely swam on. At last he tried putting his feet down. His toes touched soft mud. A few yards farther his feet found firm sand, and he waded ashore.

He glanced back and saw the tiny figure of his sister standing on the high point of Middle Hump, watching him. When he waved she waved back, then went inside the shack as he had told her to do.

Jeff made a quick tour of East Hump. It was like his and Trudy's island only smaller, a sandbar a hundred feet long with a fringe of waving beach grass down the middle. He found no footprints; apparently nobody ever came to the barren island. He searched for treasure — treasure being anything that would help him and Trudy and Sarge survive. He found only the usual dried seaweed and shells and the bedraggled carcass of a gull. He settled down to wait at the eastern point, under the lee of a low sandbank. Bridgeton Harbor's main channel swung within three hundred yards of the spot where he sat.

Minutes seemed endless. Jeff had absolutely nothing to do except fume and worry. When he held up his hands, he noticed that they twitched nervously. Panic lurked at the back of his mind, ready to pounce. He told himself, "We'll be all right. Nobody starves or dies of thirst in only three days. Nothing worse can happen than has happened already."

No matter how often he told himself this, though, he still wasn't convinced. He began to hate the loneliness of East Hump.

It was a wonderful relief to hear the putt-putt of a gasoline engine, and he leaped up. A fishing boat was swinging around the point, following the channel. She was in close enough for Jeff to make out the peeling paint and scars on her side. One man stood at the wheel steering, the other was bent over the engine.

Jeff sucked his breath in and bellowed, "Hey!"

The man at the wheel glanced that way, and Jeff jumped up and down to call attention to himself. "Hey, come in! Come over here!"

The steerer spoke to his mate, who straightened up and looked too. "We're marooned!" Jeff shouted.

They waved, but the boat kept on its course. Jeff yelled and swung his arms until it was beyond the sound of his voice. He made out the name *Serafina* on the stern.

Tears of rage stung his eyes. "Stupid jerks!" he shouted after the fishermen. But he guessed that at such a distance his voice sounded like the thin cry of a sandpiper. They couldn't make out the words.

Maybe the next time the men would have better ears. Two more boats were heading in, homeward-bound for the night. Jeff stood on the low sand-bank, so he would show against the sky. He waited until the first boat came close, then bellowed as loudly as he could. The man on deck didn't even glance over. The second boat came abreast of East Hump. Jeff's voice was hoarse by this time and his throat ached, but he yelled and yelled, "Hey, hey, hey!" A young boy sprawled on the cabin waved back. The man at the wheel paid no attention.

How could they be so dumb and so blind? Weren't they even interested enough to see whether there was a boat drawn up on the shore? How did they think Jeff had gotten there?

He scanned the Sound. No more boats were in sight. The indifference of the fishermen was more than he could bear, and in a rage Jeff ran around the island, shouting all the bad words he knew at the wheeling gulls.

At last, out of breath and panting, he stopped to let his heart quiet down. All he wanted was to get back to the other island, to the shack and the company of Trudy and Sarge. The tide had turned, the sun was sinking in the west. He forced himself to lie still, to gather strength for the long swim. When his heart stopped pounding and the weakness in his legs went away, he walked into the water and started swimming.

He had to float and rest more often this time. Hunger and thirst and disappointment and rage against the fishermen had weakened him. He reached the halfway point. The harbor was emptying into the Sound as the tide went out. Jeff swam hard, afraid he was using the last of his strength, more afraid he might get a cramp and be helplessly carried out to sea.

He reached quieter water and rested for a long time, his arms out straight to balance him. He ached all over and his heart was pounding again, so hard he felt his chest might burst.

"Jeff, Jeff!" It was Trudy calling. Sure enough, at this distance her thin voice did sound like a sandpiper's. He lifted one arm to let her know he heard, then doggedly swam on. He was so exhausted by this time he didn't care very much whether he made it or not. Drowning, just letting go, seemed like rather a pleasant prospect.

Finally his feet touched. All his strength was gone, and he fought with his arms to push the water away. A few feet farther in he stumbled and went under. Green water filled his mouth and eyes.

Trudy's small, strong arms were around him, helping him in. She half carried him up the shore and there Jeff collapsed, his face in the hot sand,

choking and sobbing for breath. Trudy knelt beside him, helplessly patting his shoulder.

Finally he managed to get hold of himself, and sat up. "It's all right, kid," he whispered.

"You mustn't ever, ever try that again," Trudy said in a scared little voice.

5

ON THAT WEDNESDAY, as the day waned, hope-lessness took possession of them. The sun lingered late, shining through the smoke of the city. Heat shimmered and eddied over the jagged outline of Bridgeton. Jeff recovered from his hard swim, and they moved to the harbor side of the island. They didn't speak; they just watched dully for the rescue boat that didn't come.

Trudy stirred herself to dig away the dry sand with her hands to the wet sand underneath, making a hollow to lie in. Jeff crouched nearby with his arms folded around the parcel. Sarge lay on his side, his tongue hanging out. His puzzled eyes seemed to be blaming his humans for his misery.

Jeff finally roused up. "Do you want your cookie?" he asked.

Trudy was having trouble speaking. Her skin was fiery red now. She tried to wet her lips. Finally she answered, "I couldn't swallow it. Maybe I could eat a little banana, but I couldn't even eat that if Sarge was watching."

"We've only got two, and they've seen their best days," Jeff said. "We'll eat the worst one tonight and save the better one for the morning. I guess we'd both feel better if we shared with Sarge."

He felt around in the sand and found a clean shell to use as a knife. Sarge heard the rustle of the paper bag and came over and planted himself in front of them. Jeff carefully cut the rottener banana in three parts. They peeled off the brown skin. Sarge accepted his share and swallowed it in one bite. For the first time that day his tail wagged.

It wasn't much of a supper, but the sweet, moist banana loosened their tongues. "You're pretty sure Gram didn't find the suitcases, aren't you?" Trudy asked.

"Let's not go into that."

"All right. Can we talk about what we'll eat when we get home? I think I'll have a dozen bananas!"

But Jeff didn't feel like talking about food. "You didn't find anything we could open the cans with?" he asked.

"No."

"We'll look some more before it gets dark."

"I bet they had a hot day in the city," Trudy commented.

Somehow, being reminded of the city and all the people in it set fire to Jeff's rage again. He said savagely, "I hope they fried!"

"Why? What's the matter?" Trudy asked, surprised.

"They haven't got any brains. Why haven't they got any brains? The men on those boats didn't care; they wouldn't even bother to come in to find out what was wrong. How about the police — don't they ever patrol this harbor? And what about Mom and Dad? Why don't they call Gram to find out how we are?"

What he meant of course was, "Why doesn't somebody care?" It seemed unbelievable to Jeff that nobody in the whole world cared enough about him and Trudy to know they were in deep trouble.

Trudy said, "Jeff, it's nobody's fault."

"What do you mean, it's nobody's fault? Look at you! You look as though you're burning up with fever, and there's not a blasted thing I can do about it. You're stupid too, that's what's the matter with you. Ahhh, you make me sick!" He jumped to his feet and started off.

Trudy called after him, "You make me sick too. You've got no call to be mad at me!" Jeff kept going.

He stalked along the shore that was their prison. Sarge followed. He saw Sarge stop to drink at a pool of salt water the tide had left. What did Jeff care if the dumb dog got sick and died? The worry of taking care of his sister was just about all he could manage.

His anger seemed to burn away the hunger that gnawed at his stomach and the thirst that ached in his throat. He reached the end of the island and shouted his rage at the mainland. Over there, thousands of brainless people were stuffing their faces with good food and drinking up water. Letting it run out of the faucet as though water was nothing. As though water couldn't save the lives of a couple of kids stuck on a stinking island right within sight of the city.

After a while the anger burned itself out, and Jeff was left feeling empty. Hunger and thirst filled that emptiness all too quickly. He stumbled with weakness when he turned back to find Trudy. He had to tell the kid he was sorry.

She was kneeling in the doorway of the shack when he came up. "I'm sorry," he said gruffly.

"Oh, that's all right."

"What are you doing?"

"I'm taking another look for the can opener."

Jeff got down on his knees too. "Let's divide it up. You do one side, I'll do the other, and we'll sift all the sand."

"Doing something is better than doing nothing," Trudy said.

This seemed to Jeff like a very bright statement, and he glanced at his sister with new respect.

He set the parcel on the high shelf, and carefully began to explore with his hands. Whenever he and Trudy were doing a thing together this way, it had always meant a great deal to Jeff to win. He always had to beat Trudy. Now, while he scrabbled around on his knees, sifting the sand on his side of the shack, he caught himself wishing that *she* would be the one to find the can opener. That was a pretty weird thing for him to be wishing, it seemed to him.

It turned out that way. Trudy gave a cry and held up a rusted opener.

This was the first good thing that had happened to them in two days, and they acted kind of silly with joy. Jeff grabbed one of the tin cans and rushed out, and was just about to try the opener on it when he stopped.

Trudy hung over him. "What's the matter? I can't wait to see what we've got!"

"It's liquid," Jeff said. "It must be some kind of juice. We've got to pour it into something, to keep it. I'll wash out the Thermos. Before we fill it, though, we ought to cool the can. Come on!"

They crossed the wet sand to the water's edge. Trudy rolled the precious can on the sandy bottom to cool it. Jeff rinsed the Thermos, sloshed clean salt water around in it, rinsed it again, and held it upside down to dry. "Do you know something?" he said happily. "After this we'll never again take food for granted. We'll appreciate everything that Mother cooks!"

The word "Mother" made Trudy's eyes fill, and her head drooped. She got hold of herself quickly. "I guess that's right," she said steadily. She added, "Jeff, I do think you're awfully smart."

"Why? It was my stupidity that got us into this mess."

They stared at each other. For the first time in his life, Jeff was admitting he had been wrong. Then they laughed. It wasn't the mean laughter of making fun of each other; it was the good laughter of sharing.

"I mean you were smart to be so careful," Trudy explained. "Almost anybody else would have opened the can and drunk some right away. But now it'll stay cool in the Thermos. What do you suppose it is?"

"I wish it was pineapple juice."

"That would be lovely, but I wouldn't mind if it was prune juice or even tomato."

"And there's another can after we drink this one! I guess it's cool enough. Do you think the great moment has arrived?" Jeff asked, grinning.

Trudy scrambled to her feet. "I'm going up the beach, and when you've poured it, then call me. I want to be surprised."

"You're nuts," Jeff said, and watched her go capering up the beach. It was almost dark now, but he saw her fling her arms wide, dancing over the dry sand. "I hope it's not sour," he thought. Trudy's disappointment would be more than he could face.

He made two holes in the rusty top of the can and put his nose to it. It smelled like fresh tomato juice. With great care not to spill a drop, he poured it into the quart Thermos. He poured back a little into the clean plastic cup and tasted it.

He had never been a great lover of tomato juice, but now he realized that nothing in the world had ever tasted so good. He filled the cup. "Come on back," he called. "The party's ready."

She took the cup, closed her eyes, and drank it

64

in little sips. "I bless the duck hunters who left it here," she said, and it sounded like a small prayer.

They gave Sarge a half cup of the precious liquid. "Just enough to wet his whistle," Trudy said with a giggle. Then Jeff suggested that they go to bed. Full dark had come.

He couldn't face sleeping inside the shack. The memory of the rats dropping on him was too vivid. They spread the two blankets on the sand. Sarge sprawled nearby. The taste of the tomato juice had puzzled him, and he looked at his master and mistress as though he thought they were crazy for liking such stuff.

Jeff had felt sleepy while they were getting ready, spreading the blankets and wrapping the food and the Thermos tightly in his jacket. They lay down, Jeff clutching the bundle. Right away he was wide awake again.

He turned his head, and by starshine saw that his sister's eyes were open too. Neither spoke. At last Jeff asked, "Why don't you go to sleep? Time goes faster that way."

"I was thinking that now we've got the tomato juice, tomorrow won't be so bad," Trudy said. "Tomorrow morning we'll have done two nights. There'll be only Thursday and Thursday night and part of Friday."

She sounded so confident, Jeff didn't feel like reminding her that their rescue on Friday wasn't as sure as she thought. Gram might wait all day for them, and not call the folks in New Millbrook until Friday night to ask why they hadn't come.

He tried to sound as confident as Trudy did. "We might be rescued tomorrow," he told her. "I've thought of something we can do in the morning. We can make a big SOS in the sand. Then if a plane goes over, the pilot might see it and we'd be rescued right away."

"We haven't seen a plane since we've been here," Trudy reminded him.

"I suppose that's because the airport is north of the city, so they don't go over the harbor. But one might stray off course or something."

"Anyway, it's a great idea." Trudy's voice sounded funny. Her teeth were chattering.

"You're not scared of the rats, are you?" Jeff asked. "I don't believe they'll bother us out here in the open."

"No, it's not the rats. I just can't stop shaking, I'm so cold."

Jeff spread his blanket over her. She moved over to make room for him, and they lay closer, the bundle between them. Jeff felt her body jerking. Her teeth were really rattling together.

He hoped she would stop shaking, and finally she did, but then she threw the blanket off. "I can't stand it, it's so hot," she said like a fussing child.

His hand touched hers and he jumped, for hers felt as though it was on fire. He realized then that her sunburn had made her really ill.

It was useless to try to sleep. Jeff said, "Try to get your mind off how awful you feel, and think of something else."

Trudy promised meekly, "All right, I'll try."

They talked about the stars, and located the Big Dipper, which was the only group Jeff knew. They talked about spaceships, and how men would get to the moon. But Trudy broke into Jeff's learned discussion of solid fuels and rockets. "Oh Jeff, I feel so awfully sick!"

"Have you blistered?"

"I guess so. The pain in my arms is something terrible."

He stared out over the dark water, trying to think of something to do. A channel marker blinked red, like a red eye. He felt terror rising in him again. He was afraid it would get the better of him and he would go to pieces, and suddenly he stood up.

"Where are you going?" Trudy asked.

"Nowhere."

"Jeff, please do something. I'll die I guess, I hurt so!"

Jeff felt as though the top of his head would blow off. "Stop talking like a sap!" he shouted at her. "Nobody ever died of sunburn. Stop being such a baby!"

He began to run, longing to be anywhere as long as it was away from his sister. He reached the end of the island and stopped, staring across at the sleeping town of West Bridgeton, where Gram lived. Fear and helpless anger were so mixed up in him he couldn't get hold of a right thought. What if Trudy did die?

Sarge had trailed him. Now by the dim light Jeff saw Sarge's head go up, and the dog shot off into the marsh grass. He barked sharply. A squeal of pure anguish followed, a death sound in the grass. That squeal sort of hung on the silent night air. Then Sarge came trotting back, his head up. He came straight to Jeff and laid something at his feet.

Jeff bent to see, and shuddered. It was one of the rats. He leaned over to pick it up by the tail, to fling it far out into the water. Sarge seized it and ran off.

Sick at his stomach, Jeff slowly made his way along the beach. Trudy was tottering to meet him. "What was that awful sound?" she asked.

"Sarge killed one of the rats."

"Did you get it away from him?"

"No, he's eating it."

"Ugh." Trudy swayed, and he caught her and led her back to the blanket. She seemed to be out of her head, blabbering, "Don't leave me again. I'm sorry I'm so much trouble, but please don't go off and leave me."

He helped her down, and folded the other blanket and put it under her head for a pillow. Then he took off his shirt and wrung it out in cold

salt water and spread it over her burning arms.

Jeff spent the rest of the night walking back and
forth to the water, wetting the shirt, covering
Trudy's arms and legs, sitting by her while her
body heat dried the cloth.

The tide went out, and then he carried handfuls
of soft mud and spread that over her. She fussed
about the smell, but he told her to be quiet, promising they would wash the mud off in the morning.

She dozed while he was taking care of her, and
at dawn fell into a deep sleep. Jeff felt of her skin.
Her legs and face felt normal again. Her arms were
hot, and swollen with great water blisters, but the
rest of her body was all right and her fever was
down.

He stretched out on the sand beside her, shivering in the cool dawn air. He wrapped both arms
around the clumsy parcel of food and slept.

6

ON THURSDAY MORNING they were awakened from their brief sleep by rain just beginning to fall. They gathered up the blankets and staggered to the shack, groggy with weariness.

Gray clouds were boiling in heavily from the east. Despite the dirty weather, the fishing boats were going out, rounding East Hump. Jeff recognized the *Serafina,* the boat he had yelled at the day before. He growled "Yahh!" at it now — not that that did much good.

He realized then that his wits were getting dull, to stand growling after fishermen who couldn't hear him. He should be rejoicing for the rain, for rain meant the end of thirst.

He recalled a war movie he had seen on television. Sailors from a bombed ship were struggling to stay alive in a rubber boat. Rain fell, and they had nothing to catch it in, so they soaked their clothes, wrung out the salt water, and sucked them when they were sodden with fresh rain.

He and Trudy were better off than those sailors, for they had a tin can for catching water. It occurred to Jeff too that clean, soft rain might be good for Trudy's burns, and he ordered her to stay outside. She huddled by the door, shivering. "How are your legs?" he asked.

"They're all right. It's my arms."

"So I gave you pretty good advice when I made you wear your dungarees yesterday."

"Okay, so you gave me good advice. But look at my arms." Trudy stuck them out.

Jeff was shocked. Her thin little arms were swollen with great, angry blisters. No wonder she had had such an awful night. The fiery red of her face had turned to tan. He laid his hand on it and it felt cool.

She sat in the rain looking pathetic, expecting Jeff to come up with some magic cure for her hurts. Tears mixed with rain ran down her face.

Jeff couldn't bear to watch her, so he got busy, talking and working, trying to take her mind off her troubles. The evening before he had carefully rinsed out the can which had held the tomato juice. This tin can was a real treasure when they had so few possessions. He set it outside to fill. Trudy managed a wan smile, hearing the musical tinkle of rain in it.

He called her into the shack for breakfast. He divided one cookie, and they finished the tomato juice in the Thermos. The dog came for his hand-out, but Jeff told him that the rat he had eaten during the night would have to keep him going.

The last banana had been a sad-looking object the night before. Now it was dissolved into brown jelly. Jeff divided that into thirds, and Sarge got his share. Neither of them begrudged it to him.

Fortified by a cup of juice, half a cookie, and a third of a rotten banana, the best meal they had eaten in two days, Jeff felt full of energy. "Do you want to come?" he asked Trudy.

"Where?"

"I'm going to make the SOS in the sand. If any planes are up today, they'll be flying low under the clouds. This might be the very day they'd see a marker."

Trudy followed him, holding her arms stiffly in front of her. Her teeth chattered, but today it was the damp cold, not fever, that caused it. She looked tired from lack of sleep, and her face was dirty and her hair was ragged and dull, but she wasn't sick. Jeff felt sort of lightheaded to be relieved of that particular worry.

The tide had been high around five and now was ebbing to its low, exposing the mud flats. All his life Jeff had liked this ripe, salty smell. After two solid days of it, though, he knew that if he never smelled it again, it would be too soon.

He chose the widest stretch on the north beach and cleared it above the waterline, carrying off driftwood and tangles of grass and junk. Then, figuring it would be good for Trudy to keep busy and forget her troubles, he asked her to collect wet seaweed.

They tramped up and down the island in the pouring rain, and soon had a high pile of brown weed. Jeff shuffled a pattern with his feet, an S, an O, an S, in letters twenty feet high. Carrying armfuls of weed, he and Trudy arranged it along the lines he had marked.

He surveyed his work with satisfaction. "The rain will keep it wet, and it'll show up dark against the sand," he explained. "If the pilot of a plane sees it, he'll be honor-bound to fly lower and investigate. People have to pay attention to an SOS. Then, if he's got a brain in his head, he'll see that there isn't any boat drawn up on the shore and he'll guess somebody's marooned."

"I'm soaked to the skin," Trudy complained. "I'm freezing. My sneakers slosh."

He could have snapped, "When you're hot you want to be cold, and when you're cold you want to be hot." Instead he said mildly, "That's all right, Sis. At least your sunburn is getting a good rest."

"How's yours?"

"It doesn't amount to anything. My skin's tough."

They walked back to the shack. It seemed in a peculiar way like going home. "Hey, do you know something? We don't fight all the time now," Trudy remarked.

A crooked smile twisted Jeff's mouth. Smiling didn't come easily for him. "Just don't get the idea you're my favorite character I'd like to be marooned with," he warned. "I can think of movie stars I'd rather have!"

Their tin can was half full, and they drank it all and set the can out to fill again. The rain continued to come down steadily. "Did you ever think water would taste so good?" Trudy asked. "When we were little kids we didn't think we could drink just plain water out of the faucet. We had to have milk or soda or something."

"When we were kids — that was only three days ago," Jeff said.

"Do you feel a lot older?"

"I sure do. We're aging fast! But we've learned a lot, too. Figure it out. We've been stuck here two full days. This afternoon it'll be forty-eight hours, and that's an awful lot of hours. We're still alive, we're doing okay. We could stick it out awhile longer if we had to."

"Until tomorrow," Trudy said.

She waited for Jeff's answer. It didn't come, and she asked, "We'll be found tomorrow for sure, won't we?"

"Yes," he said, "we'll be rescued tomorrow."

"Wouldn't it be something if we still had food and water left when the people come? You're as smart as Robinson Crusoe any old day. I bet you'd figure out something even if the cookies were gone and we still didn't get rescued," Trudy said confidently.

"We'd try that Boy Scout trick of rubbing sticks together and making a fire," he told her. "What would we cook?"

"A fish."

"How would we catch it?"

"We'd find a bent pin," Trudy said. "Don't forget, we found a can opener when we needed one."

For no good reason Trudy had cheered up, and Jeff had no desire to cut her down to size. He kept glancing at her. She shivered constantly, and sometimes her teeth chattered. She looked kind of awful, not having washed for days, but she was a real person. Trudy wasn't just a nothing, a nobody. She wasn't just a nuisance who had moved in on Jeff's family and taken all the attention away from him.

He had disliked her ever since he could remember, because she had spoiled his chances of being an only child. Now it occurred to him that maybe his mother and father hadn't done so badly to get a daughter and give him a sister.

They sat together on the bunk. The dampness made the mattress smell riper than ever. Sarge joined them, threw himself down, let out a big sigh, and closed his eyes. Jeff thought how lucky dogs were. If they had nothing better to do they could always sleep. Time went faster if you were a dog. The hours didn't drag.

He thought of stretching out on the bunk and doing the same, but knew it was useless. He tried reading the old yellow newspapers they had found in the shack, but couldn't keep his mind on the words. Acute hunger came and went, but the gnawing in his stomach was steady. If he closed his eyes and dozed, the gnawing would soon wake him.

At least the dry mouth and sore throat of thirst were gone. Jeff stuck his arm outside for the tin can. They each took a good drink, and Jeff poured what was left into the Thermos.

The bunk shook with Trudy's trembling. "Why don't you wrap up in the blankets?" he asked.

"They're too damp."

"In your case it's better to be too cold than too hot. How do your arms feel?"

She solemnly inspected her blisters. "They hurt, but the fire's going out of them, it seems like."

Nervousness seized Jeff. He couldn't sit and watch her shiver any longer, and jumped up. "I haven't gone beachcombing today."

"What's to find?" she asked.

"The tide might have washed up something pretty good. You don't have to come. Stay here and hold the fort."

Sarge got to his feet, but Trudy put her hand on his collar. "You stay with me, dog." Sarge wrestled to get free, but Trudy clung to him.

"You're not scared, are you?" Jeff asked.

"No, but if I'm going to take care of the cookies, then this dog has to stay and watch out for the rats."

"There's probably only one left, and it wouldn't attack in broad daylight. If Sarge comes with me, maybe he'll kill it."

"Just the same, I want him to stay," Trudy said stubbornly.

Jeff didn't argue. Trudy had a right to her own ideas. She wasn't lying down and quitting; she was measuring up pretty darn well.

Jeff remembered his father saying once, "You

think you're entitled to respect because you're older, Jeff. Your sister is entitled to respect too." Jeff walked along, his head down against the rain, thinking that maybe his father had been right about that. So his father could have been right about other things too.

That was something that being stuck on an island did for you. Maybe you went kind of stir-crazy, walking around and around it, but you did catch up on your thinking, that was for sure.

During the past two days he had collected several piles of driftwood. It wasn't much good to him since he had no matches, but it gave him something to do. He thought now, "When Trudy and I come over here again, we'll have plenty of wood to make a fire." Then he decided, "We'll never do that. If we ever get back on *terra firma,* I'll never set foot in any boat again."

Hunger drove him. Maybe it wasn't too smart to burn up his energy on a useless job, but nevertheless he dragged all the branches, broken crates, lengths of board, up to the high ridge of the island. The last tide had made him a present of two heavy, waterlogged timbers held together by a rusted bolt. He added those to his big pile.

He scuffed at a heap of sodden seaweed, and when he turned it over discovered that underneath the strands were dry. He stuffed some of this crisp seaweed inside his shirt, where it scratched. He ran back to the shack, for he had decided to try the Boy Scout trick.

He was in a gay mood when he dashed in, and Trudy's face brightened. She had wrapped the damp blanket around her, and Jeff saw that tears had furrowed her dirty face.

He pretended not to see that she had been crying. "We're going to find out whether there's anything to that stuff you learn in Scouting," he told her. "We're going to make a fire."

The newspapers were carefully folded and dry on the shelf. Jeff thought it was lucky that they had learned early to take care of things. The broken orange crate in the corner was also dry. Jeff patted the sand smooth. Then he tore a sheet of newspaper into small pieces and crumpled them. He crumbled the seaweed between his hands and sifted it over the paper. "Now what do we do?" he asked.

Trudy was grinning at the mere thought of fire. "I think you're supposed to have a round stick with a string to make it turn," she told him.

"We haven't got a piece of string. We'll try rubbing two sticks."

He broke off some thin wood from the orange

crate and cut his hand on a wire, but impatiently shook off the blood. He split the pieces into narrow strips and laid them beside him, ready in case a flame ignited the paper. Then he broke the thin round stick which had held the crate's cover closed, and crouched over his pile of paper and seaweed and began to rub.

He rubbed and rubbed and rubbed. The sticks felt warmer where they crossed each other. He kept up a steady chatter, telling Trudy how cozy it was going to be when they had a fire to sit over, and that maybe they'd catch some crabs and cook them. Instead of agreeing, Trudy looked frightened, watching him.

His back began to hurt from his crouching position, and his arms ached. Trudy said, "Jeff, it isn't working, so don't get yourself all tired out."

"It will work," he said. "It's got to work. If a bunch of Indians and Boy Scouts can do it, then we can too." He went on rubbing, and it seemed to him as though his and Trudy's only chance of survival lay in creating a puff of smoke that would turn into a flame and ignite the paper.

"Jeff, please," Trudy begged.

"Please what?"

"Stop it, Jeff. You look awfully funny. Are you sick or something? You act kind of crazy."

That made him terribly angry. He didn't stop working with the sticks, but he shouted, "There's nothing crazy about making a fire! There's nothing crazy about trying to stay alive! What if Gram doesn't call the folks to tell them we didn't come? Then how long will we be stuck here? What makes you so sure they'll know where we are? They might never think of our going out in the boat. Don't you ever think things through, you nitwit? We might be here for weeks before it occurs to somebody to look and see if Gram's boat is missing!"

All the time he was yelling at her Jeff had kept on furiously rubbing the sticks. Trudy let out a sobbing cry of terror and clutched his arm. "Jeff, please, please stop it! You're sick."

Suddenly the strength drained out of Jeff's arms. He snapped the sticks and threw them down. Then he jerked away from Trudy and staggered out into the rain. When he reached the beach he fell, sprawling on the sand, his face on his arms.

Trudy hovered over him, crying in a broken-hearted way. Jeff went completely to pieces, sobbing until his throat throbbed like a wound and his head felt as though it was bursting. He lost himself in terror. It was as though he entered and disappeared in a dark tunnel that had no ending.

84

7

WHEN JEFF GOT CONTROL OF HIMSELF he was lying in the rain, his sister crouched beside him, smoothing back his hair with her hand. He still shuddered with sobs, but he croaked, "I'm sorry."

"That's the second time you've said that. You said it yesterday too," Trudy mentioned.

He rolled over and sat up. "I guess I scared the wits out of you."

"Yes, you did. Boy, you went all to pieces."

He didn't want to look at her. He was shocked and ashamed, and also he was angry with himself. He had handed his sister a weapon she could use against him. "I'll never hear the end of this," he thought. Trudy would use this knowledge that he had broken down and cried like a baby.

"Let's forget it," she said now.

"You won't forget it," he mumbled. "Just as soon as we get off this blasted island you'll tell some-body."

Her hurt showed in her face. "Jeff, I thought we were beginning to act like friends," she said.

He made no answer, just looked away.

Their nerves were shot, that was the trouble. Being so hungry would do that, and getting sun-burned and then freezing in the rain didn't help. Jeff stuffed his hands in his pockets because they shook so.

He didn't want to think about them, but he couldn't get his mind off the cookies. If he ate what was left, it would stop the gnawing in his stomach and give him strength to keep going. They were big, delicious coconut cookies. They would make a real meal.

Trudy had wandered up the beach. Jeff slowly followed her, because he didn't want to be left alone with the cookies. "Why don't you stay inside the shack?" he asked when he came up with her.

"We can't get any wetter than we are."

They aimlessly rounded the island and came to the north side. Through the slanting rain they could see the city and the turnpike, the cars shooting along like beetles. Again Jeff had the feeling of no longer belonging in the real world, of being stuck on another planet. At times like this he wondered if help would ever come.

If he really gave up hope, then he would have had it. He would be finished, he would dissolve into a whining baby. He shook himself. It was an hour since they had spoken, and this silence between him and Trudy ought not to go on. He had to say something. "We're certainly no great shakes as fire makers," he said.

"Was that what upset you?" Trudy asked. "Jeff, I don't believe anybody could make a fire without better stuff than we had. Jeff, honestly I'd never tell, about your crying and all."

"Let's skip it."

"You didn't have any right to say I'd blab. I think you're great. I mean, I don't mind being stuck with you on this awful island."

Trudy was waiting for some sort of an answer from him, but Jeff couldn't give it. He was too afraid he might cry again. She waited, then walked on alone.

He wanted to be alone too, and yet he also wanted to be with her. He trailed a few feet behind. She stopped at the point, staring across to West Hump. "The tide's coming in," she said. "What time would that make it?"

"If that crazy sun would come out, we could tell.

Low tide was around eleven, so that would make it about noon now."

"Only half of this day is gone."

"I'm going to try to swim to West Hump this afternoon." Jeff surprised himself, for he hadn't given this idea any real thought at all. Suddenly he hated this prison island so much he couldn't bear it. They couldn't be any worse off behind walls ten feet thick. The only way to escape the island was to swim away from it.

"There isn't any wind," he went on, "and I'd only have to swim it one way. I could make it, with no wind to kick up waves. If I got to West Hump, I could make it to the mainland easy. I'd get through the marsh all right. I'd come out at the end of Crescent Avenue, and Gram's house is only five or six blocks from there. I'd borrow a boat and come right back for you —"

Trudy stopped him by seizing his arm. "I won't be left here alone! You'd be drowned and I'd be left here forever. Jeff, I can't stay alone, I can't, I can't, I can't!"

It was Trudy's turn to lose control. Her eyes blazed in her distorted little face. Jeff put his hands on her shoulders and shook her. That did no good; she just kept yelling, "I can't, I can't!" He thought of slapping her, for he'd heard that was a sure way to stop a person who was having hysterics.

He couldn't do it. His hand wouldn't obey him, and he couldn't hit her. Instead he pulled her against him.

She wrapped her skinny arms around his neck and hung on, pressing her face against the shoulder of his wet shirt. Jeff thought, shocked. "What if anybody saw me hugging my sister?"

The result of what he was doing was startling, though, for Trudy quieted right down. She pressed against him as though she was getting her nerve back just from touching him. He patted her back clumsily. "That's okay," he whispered.

Soon she did break away. Maybe she was as embarrassed as he was. "You sure got a drip when you got me for a sister," she mumbled.

They wandered back to the shack. They found the tin can full and drank all they wanted, and gave Sarge what was left. Jeff set the can out to fill again. They were rich now, as far as drinking water went.

"Do you want a piece of cookie?" Jeff asked.

They both felt so queer, they acted queerly. How could they snarl at each other now, after what had happened? Besides, Jeff was feeling grateful to Trudy. If she hadn't thrown her fit, he would

89

have had to try swimming to West Hump. The mere thought of the swim had terrified him as soon as he had suggested it.

Trudy said, "No thank you. I'll have my cookie for supper." She asked then, "Would it bother you to talk about food?"

"No, I guess not."

She perked up. "I'm going to have a baked potato with lots of butter."

"I guess I'll settle for a steak and a bowl of Gram's pea soup," Jeff said, falling in with the game.

"I suppose Gram will give us just about anything we ask for."

"She'd jolly well better!" Jeff blustered. "The way she's left us out here, she's got some tall explaining to do!"

Trudy began to giggle. She laughed and laughed and couldn't stop. Jeff snorted, but soon he was laughing too. Something in his heart let go. He felt free, he felt good. Trudy darted away and he chased her. They ran in circles, capering in the pouring rain.

Finally Trudy collapsed on the beach, still giggling. Then she began to cough and couldn't stop. Jeff pounded her on the back, but that did no good, and he raised her arms high to let air into her lungs.

She choked and sputtered, but finally her breathing became easier. She started to giggle again weakly.

Jeff motioned her to be silent. Listening hard, he could hear a motor overhead, coming their way. A small plane appeared between layers of cloud, then vanished. They could still hear it, and Jeff shouted, "Hey, we're down here! Hey, come down!" The plane droned out of hearing.

The afternoon dragged, but they killed it somehow. They could talk about the plane now. Had the pilot seen their SOS or hadn't he? Trudy kept an eye on the tide, to tell the time. As she did every day at high tide, she watched the harbor for a rescue boat.

She wasn't too disappointed though, because she didn't have any doubt whatsoever that tomorrow was R Day. Tomorrow was Friday, Rescue Day. Tomorrow Gram would be watching for all the Pennells. When they didn't come, Gram would telephone to find out if they had changed their plans. Their mother would answer, would tell Gram the Bensons had brought the children down, and right away everybody would get all upset.

Dad or Gram or somebody would instantly guess, "The kids went out in the boat." They'd probably all worry about the fact that the two of them might have been drowned, but then somebody would mention their special island. Gram would ask a neighbor to row over to Middle Hump to rescue them. If Gram notified the police instead, that might be even better. The rescue would be a big thing, and Jeff and Trudy would get their names in the paper.

This was the way Trudy figured it. She had been over and over it so many times there wasn't a doubt in her mind that this would happen tomorrow. She couldn't see any holes in the argument.

Jeff could see holes in it big enough to drive a truck through, but he kept silent about his doubts.

Trudy's cough grew worse as the day wore on. She huddled on the bunk, her eyes dull. She didn't laugh or even smile any more. Jeff tried to get her interested in opening the other can. They hoped for pineapple juice, but it turned out to be tomato again. With a quarter of a cookie apiece, they made out a supper that wasn't too bad. They saved the other half cookie for a going-to-bed treat.

The sound of Trudy's coughing was getting on Jeff's nerves. He wrapped her up tight in both damp blankets. The scratchiness hurt her blistered arms and she threw them off.

He left her to make another tour of the island. The rain had slackened to a drizzle. For a long time he watched the traffic zooming along the turnpike across the harbor. Drivers had turned their parking lights on early. The flowing cars looked like strings of golden beads.

As dark came down, the harbor and sky and sea blended into one grayness, and that awful feeling of being alone on the planet seized Jeff. He whistled for Sarge and turned toward home.

Home was the shack, of course. The thought crossed Jeff's mind that the shack seemed like home because Trudy was there. If anybody had told him two days ago he would hurry to get back to his sister because he missed her, Jeff would have told that person he was crazy and ought to see a head doctor.

She was still huddled on the bunk, shivering. He touched her hand and it was hot. "Oh my gosh, are you going to be sick again?" he asked.

"Gee, I don't know, Jeff."

"Do you hurt?"

"My chest does, sort of, but it's just a cold."

"Maybe tomorrow at this time you'll be in a nice dry bed, and Gram will be bringing you hot cocoa and stuff."

"There's no maybe about it," Trudy said hoarsely.

He didn't answer.

"There isn't, is there?"

"No, of course not." Jeff said abruptly, "Look, I'm going around the island one final time, and then we'll get ready for the night."

He was hoping for a gleam of red in the west, remembering the saying, "Red sky at night, sailors' delight." But there was no promise of a clear tomorrow. The sky was still hidden by heavy, scudding clouds. At the east end he waited for the fishing boats to swing round East Hump.

The *Serafina* and the other boats didn't come while he watched. Since hope was just about the only thing that kept Jeff going, he had been nursing the small hope all day that the fishermen would see him tonight, and one of them would have the brains to wonder why a kid was still on the island.

He dawdled around, peering out across the harbor. The boats still didn't come, so he walked home to the shack, and his heart felt like a big lump of lead. The long night ahead seemed like more than he could face.

Dark was settling fast. He heard Trudy's coughing as he came up. Her face glimmered whitely in the dusk, and she said, "I do hope my coughing isn't going to keep you awake tonight."

Did she dread being shut up inside the shack as much as he did? If Jeff had had a choice, he would have slept on the beach despite the drizzle. He had none; he had to stay inside with Trudy.

"Don't let's ever come over here again without a flashlight," he said.

"And our toothbrushes," Trudy croaked.

"I know, my teeth feel furry too," he told her.

They divided a half cookie, each saving a corner for Sarge. They finished the tomato juice, and Jeff set the can outside, figuring the rain might come back and fill both cans. The Thermos was full of water, so they had that supply to go on.

He and Trudy had an argument about the blankets. She insisted he spread one on the sand for his bed, and he insisted that she lie on it and spread the other one over her. He won, or rather Trudy let him have his way. Her voice gave out.

Their Friday-morning cookie was all they had left. Jeff tore the bag and wrapped this precious object in a small piece of brown paper and put it in his jacket pocket, where he could keep his hand over it.

Fumbling around in the dark, they kept falling

over Sarge. He stayed close, anxious about the bits of cookie he knew they had saved for him. "Once he's fed, he won't stay with us," Jeff warned. "He hates being shut up in here with the door closed. You give him his cookie while I fix the door, and hang on to him. It's going to be pitch-dark once the door's shut, so we have to have everything ready before I close it."

"Are you keeping him in on account of the rat?"

"On account of the rat and other things. He's a nice hot dog. I mean, he's got a lot of body warmth. When the three of us are shut inside, it might get real nice and toasty in here."

Trudy gave a sob. "He might kill the rat while we're jammed in like sardines."

Jeff ordered, "Stop thinking about the rat. Think what an exciting story you'll have to tell your grandchildren when you get some."

Trudy giggled, and it was such a cheerful sound the heavy weight of Jeff's heart felt a little lighter. "Ready?" he asked.

"Ready."

She held Sarge's collar and offered his cookie. Jeff set the door in place.

Sarge whined when he found himself shut up in the small place. Then he settled down with his nose to the crack of the door. Finally he gave a slobbery sigh and slept.

There was silence for a little while. Sarge took up more than his share of the room, pressing warmly against Jeff. Trudy spoke first. "I'm going to put out my hand to see if I can touch you," she said. "Shut your eyes. I don't want to poke your eye out."

"Go ahead," he told her, and felt her small, grubby hand on his face.

"There's really nothing awful to be scared of," Trudy said.

"No. Only the dark."

"Maybe when we get home we won't fight any more. I don't really want to fight any more, Jeff."

"All right," he said soothingly, "maybe it'll be kind of dull, but we won't fight any more. Now go to sleep."

8

J EFF AWOKE ONCE TO FIND AN EYE peering through the crack over the door. He saw it was a star blinking in at him and thought, "Tomorrow will be clear and Trudy won't get pneumonia." She was coughing now in her sleep. If he could possibly manage it, he wanted to hand Trudy back to his parents alive and well.

The next time Jeff stirred, Sarge banged his tail against the bunk. This aroused Trudy from her light sleep. Jeff set the door aside.

He looked into a world of gray. Fog had rolled in, and clammy cold enveloped him as he stepped out. There wasn't a sound except the lapping of waves. Telling time by how far the tide had come in, Jeff guessed it must be about five o'clock.

Trudy joined him and they wandered aimlessly, Sarge trailing them. Fog was a new element; it shrank their entire world to a few hundred square yards of sand, forming a wall of mist that seemed as solid as the thick stone walls of a prison. Somewhere out to sea a foghorn bellowed like a cow in pain.

Trudy put her hand on Jeff's arm, and he felt her shudder. "I know," he said. "That noise will drive me nuts if it keeps up very long."

They circled Middle Hump to the west shore and sat together on the wet sand, Jeff keeping his hand over the cookie in his shirt pocket. They stared to the west where the harbor and the city ought to be.

Jeff realized slowly then that their white wall was thinning. The world was soundlessly growing larger. Now they could glance along and see their shore emerging. The fog lifted a little, to hover a few feet above the gray, glassy water.

Trudy turned to him, smiling with relief. "It's going away."

He held up his hand for silence. They heard a heavy, beating sound, far off. It came nearer, and they strained to see through the mist over their heads. "It sounds like a helicopter," Jeff said.

Trudy screamed hoarsely. Jeff yelled too, but he didn't let himself go. He didn't dare get his hopes up, and he couldn't endure the thought of Trudy suffering any more disappointments.

The sound dwindled away. "It'll be back," Trudy said.

"I hope this stupid fog is gone if it takes another swing around," Jeff agreed.

"It's somebody looking for us," she said confidently. Jeff hesitated. "It is, isn't it?" she insisted.

"I don't know, Trudy. I hope so," was all the answer he could give her.

They returned to the shack, practically tiptoeing, afraid to make a noise and miss any sound overhead. Jeff's ears began to ache, he was listening so hard.

"I wish I had a comb, so I wouldn't look so crummy when they come," Trudy fretted.

Jeff glanced at her and saw her as a stranger might, and he thought, "Gee, she's homely, with her face so dirty and her hair all scraggly." Then, seeing her with his own eyes instead of a stranger's, he thought, "Trudy's got a lot of nerve. She's okay. She's somebody, she really is."

"How do your arms feel?" he asked her.

"All right," she said quickly.

They heard the whirring again. The helicopter was coming in from the east this time. Jeff's heart pounded, for it sounded as though the pilot was making a search pattern. It passed over, still hidden.

"Look!" Trudy cried, pointing to a small patch of blue sky in the west. "I've been staring at that spot for five minutes because I thought the cloud was getting thinner. Just now the blue broke through."

"Let's hope it gets really big. They say if the blue's big enough to make a pair of Dutchman's britches, then you know it's really going to clear," Jeff said.

"We could make a pair for a little Dutch boy now!"

"It's got to be for a big Dutchman," Jeff told her.

He walked away then, for he couldn't listen for the helicopter when they were chattering. He broke into a run, fetching up on the north shore.

He thought his eardrums would burst, he was straining so hard to hear. The fog was thinning all around, and he could make out the entire shore-line now, with the city's tall buildings gleaming palely. Up there in the whiteness the chopper was passing back and forth. If only the pilot didn't give up and return to his base before the mist over the islands vanished!

No, here it came again. It flew in low from the west, and this time it was heading directly over Middle Hump. Miraculously, just then the last

shreds of fog disappeared. Jeff clearly read BRIDGETON POLICE DE-PARTMENT lettered on its side.

Trudy came running. Jeff was jumping up and down yelling like a wild man. The 'copter went over, turned back, and hovered over their heads. A man in a police uniform leaned out and waved.

The chopper settled right in the middle of the SOS, blowing sand in all directions. The pilot cut the motor, the blades stopped rotating, and the policeman jumped out.

Trudy rushed to him and threw her arms around him and clung to him. Jeff knew how she felt. The man in blue looked like an angel straight from heaven to Jeff too.

The officer hugged Trudy gently. "What's going on here?" he asked.

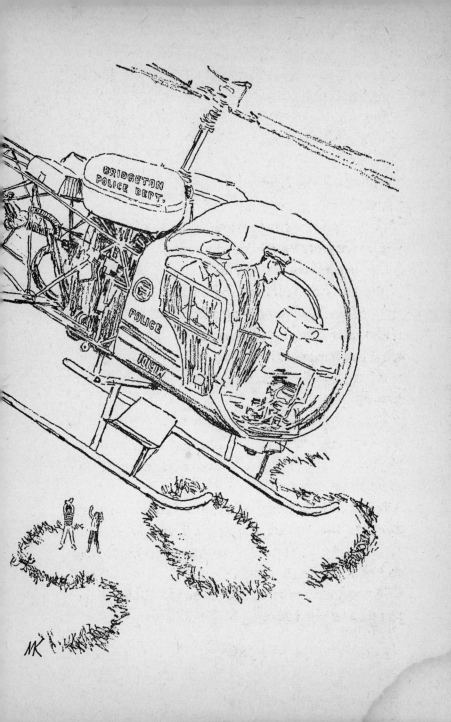

Trudy, embarrassed, let go of him and hid behind her brother. "I'm Jeffrey Pennell," Jeff stated. "This is my sister. We're sure glad to see you, mister. We've been stuck out here since last Tuesday afternoon!"

The pilot had joined them. The two officers found Jeff's statement hard to believe. "No lost children have been reported," they said. "The only reason we were searching was because a man called the police to say he flew over here yesterday and he thought he might have spotted an SOS."

"I guess we weren't reported lost because nobody missed us," Jeff told them, and explained what had happened.

OFFICER KELLY SAID, when Jeff finished, "I do believe it, now that I take a real look at you. You children look as though you'd had a rough time, especially the little girl. That's a bad cough she's got. We'd better get you to the hospital. Let's not hang around here any longer."

It turned out there was only room in the 'copter for two besides Officer Olson, the pilot. Officer Kelly ordered him to take off without delay. The pilot contacted their headquarters by radio and asked for an ambulance to meet them at Bridgeton Airport. He also requested that a police boat be sent out to pick up his fellow officer.

Officer Kelly lifted Trudy in, then patted her hand. "Don't be frightened, Trudy. I have a little girl just about your age, and she's been up with us in this machine and liked it."

Jeff had the queerest feeling as he watched the men being so gentle with his sister. He had taken care of her for three days, taken pretty darn good care of her too. Now that was over. Things would be different between him and Trudy now — maybe not worse but different, because they were going back to civilization.

Suddenly Trudy's face crumpled and she started to cry. "We can't go! Jeff, we have to stay with Sarge."

Where had the dog been through all the excitement? "Who's Sarge?" the police asked.

"There he is." Trudy pointed.

Sarge was half hidden in the beach grass, watching what was going on. Jeff started for him, and he slunk away.

"You kids go along with my partner," Officer Kelly ordered. "I'll look after the dog and bring him in with me when the boat comes."

"I don't believe you'll be able to catch him," Jeff said. "He's gotten kind of wild these past three days."

"Jeff, you've still got our last cookie," Trudy reminded him. "You could use that." Jeff climbed out of the machine.

"Look, kids, we can't waste any more time.

We've got to get you to the hospital," Officer Kelly said. "Get in, Jeff. I can manage the dog."

Trudy and Jeff looked at each other. He knew she agreed: they couldn't leave the island until they knew Sarge was going to be safe. Despite the protests of the men, Jeff started after Sarge. The dog quickened his pace, heading toward the eastern point. "His leash is hanging in the shack," Trudy called.

Officer Kelly caught up with Jeff. As they walked to the shack he questioned Jeff thoroughly. He seemed really troubled. He thought it was the fault of the police that such an incredible thing could happen, that children could be marooned within sight of a big city.

This thought had crossed Jeff's mind also, but he didn't say so. He only said, "It was all my fault. I should have left word for my grandmother, and I was the one who let the boat get away."

The policeman wasn't satisfied, but he said, "We'll let that go until later. The first job is to catch that dog."

This was easier said than done. Sarge stood at the edge of the water, his tail between his legs. Jeff guessed that the helicopter had scared him badly. He growled when the policeman approached. Jeff held the leash and told the older man to stay back.

He was sorely tempted to eat at least part of this last precious cookie, for his hunger was a sharp pain this morning. He didn't because he needed it for bait to catch the dog. Sarge's own hunger was stronger than his fear of the stranger. He grabbed the cookie, and Jeff snapped the leash on his collar.

"He's not a savage dog," he explained. "Usually he's very friendly, but he's had quite an awful time too."

"We'll get along all right," Officer Kelly assured him. "The boat will be out soon to take us off."

"The tide's on its way out," Jeff reminded him.

"We'll wait then. Don't worry, I'll take good care of your dog."

"I ought to wait with you for the boat," Jeff insisted. He was really nervous about Sarge. The big dog had never bitten anybody in his life, and Jeff didn't want him to start in on a policeman. How would he act when he saw his master abandoning him?

"No. Get in, sonny."

Sarge thrashed around, trying to twist out of his collar when they neared the helicopter. Jeff held him while Officer Kelly got on the radio to headquarters and asked his superior officer to call the children's grandmother. "Have her meet us at the hospital," he suggested.

Then he chuckled. "When you send that boat to pick me up, send some dog food along too."

His boss must have been startled by that. Officer Kelly told him, "We've got all sorts of castaways on this island, Chief, including a large and hungry German shepherd. I'll bring him to the station."

He stepped away. Sarge let out one long, lonely howl as the chopper lifted.

They were winging away over the harbor. It looked incredibly blue and beautiful in the bright morning sunshine. Jeff and Trudy looked back and saw the man and the dog on the lonely shore of Middle Hump.

Jeff had a lump in his throat. Nobody seemed to own the three islands. They were just useless piles of sand. But now he felt as though Middle Hump truly belonged to him and his sister. They were leaving behind them there a short but important piece of their lives.

10

THE PILOT BROUGHT THE 'COPTER DOWN low over the city, to give his passengers a good view. They arrived at the airport a few minutes later. An ambulance came clanging across the field to meet them.

Another car careened after it and a man jumped out. "I'm a reporter for the *Bridgeton News*," he announced. "I want to interview these two."

"Not now," Officer Olson said, and pushed him away from Jeff and Trudy and hustled them into the ambulance.

Trudy's eyes shone, and Jeff too enjoyed the fast ride into the city, the lights blinking and the sirens wailing. He was feeling better every minute, and all of a sudden he couldn't contain his happiness any longer and yelled, "Oh boy, food!"

"Have you really been on that island since

last Tuesday?" the ambulance driver asked. He sounded as though he thought the whole thing was a hoax, a stunt.

Officer Olson, who was sitting up front, answered for them. "The two kids were marooned, and you'd better believe it!"

"Sure, sure," the driver said hastily, and asked, "What do you want to eat?"

Jeff didn't have to think that over. "I'll settle for anything as long as it's a thick steak and a baked potato, with a gallon of chocolate ice cream on the side."

The ambulance backed up to the emergency entrance, and a nurse and a young doctor came out to take charge. Everyone in the busy place glanced at Jeff and Trudy curiously. Jeff was well aware that he looked like a bum. He also wondered if he smelled bad, not having bathed in several days.

The reporter they had seen at the airport rushed in, but the doctor hustled the children away. The reporter had a chance to call, "How do you feel, kids?"

"Fine!" Jeff called back.

Before he realized it was happening, he and his sister were separated. Trudy was led away by the nurse, to be cared for. The doctor kept hold of Jeff's arm, and asked as the elevator sped upward, "How do you really feel, Jeff?"

"Listen, there's nothing wrong with me that a square meal won't cure," Jeff said earnestly. "I want to see my grandmother as soon as she comes."

"You will, after we get you cleaned up and look you over."

A nurse showed Jeff into an empty room and instructed him to get into bed. It occurred to Jeff that she intended to bathe him, so he jumped out of the bed and insisted on taking his own shower. The doctor came in when he finished, gave him an examination and asked some questions, then said, "You look like a healthy specimen to me — a few pounds lighter probably, but none the worse for wear. Your clothes are being washed and dried, so the nurse will give you a robe. There's some lunch for you in your sister's room."

"How is she?"

"We'll keep her here a day or two, but as far as we can tell now she has nothing worse than sun blisters and a cold."

"I was afraid she had pneumonia."

"No. Both of you are lucky."

The doctor walked him along a corridor. A piping voice called from one of the rooms, "Jeff?"

Trudy was sitting up in bed with a tray of food in front of her. Her cheeks were pink and her hair was brushed. Jeff saw how pretty she was, now that she was clean again.

Gram jumped up from a chair to meet him. Her hat was slapped on any old way, and Jeff could tell she was all shook up. She clutched him and folded him in her arms, and he hugged her back, feeling the tears on her sweet face. "Oh darling, you've had such an awful time!"

"It wasn't so bad," he said. "Was it, Trudy?"

"No," Trudy said calmly, "it was sort of fun in a horrible kind of way, but it's just great to meet up with food again! They'll give us real food if we can keep down soup all right. Help yourself, Jeff."

He never would have believed he would get excited about chicken soup, but it tasted so good he wondered why he hadn't put it first on his list. Toast and hot cocoa disappeared rapidly. Gram hung over him, near enough to pat him.

"How did you get here, Gram?" he asked.

"The police came to the house and drove me to the hospital. Your mother and father are on their way. I don't suppose they'll ever let you visit me again," Gram said.

"Oh yes they will. What happened wasn't your

fault. I was a dope not to leave you a note, and we shouldn't have hidden the suitcases."

"The suitcases?"

He explained how he had chucked them in the bushes and forgotten about them.

"You must think me a perfect fool not to guess you had been in the house," Gram said.

"Didn't you miss the bananas or milk or cookies? That was the only other clue that would have let you know we'd been around."

"Jeff," his grandmother said, "you know I'm kind of chuckle-headed and never pay attention."

The doctor appeared. "Mrs. Pennell, a reporter wants to interview your grandchildren. If you give your permission, I'll let him come in now."

Trudy's face was radiant. "Hey, what do you know, we're IMPORTANT!" she cried, and sat up looking important.

She and Jeff shared in giving the story to the reporter. They tried to be fairly truthful, but they left out a few things. When the newsman said, "You admit you were frightened, Trudy. Tell the truth now, wasn't your brother too?"

Trudy said firmly, "No, not for a minute. He was just terrific."

It was easy for Jeff to say good things about

Trudy, about what a wonderful sport she had been. They also praised Sarge. They told how he had killed the rat, and didn't mention that he had scared them by turning mean for a little while. Loyalty stopped them. The three had shared the danger and hunger and thirst together.

The reporter closed his notebook. "Now I'll have a talk with the police. You might find a little item in tonight's paper about your adventure, kids."

Jeff went back to the other room and dressed, then said good-bye to Trudy. She didn't seem to mind being left at the hospital, for she was getting plenty of attention. Besides, her parents would soon come.

Gram asked the girl at the desk to call a taxi. Gram seemed kind of wobbly and helpless, and Jeff kept his arm around her while they waited. "Jeff," she said softly, "it was lovely to see you kiss your sister good-bye just now."

Jeff growled, "Why shouldn't I? Trudy's not so bad."

11

GRAM MOPPED TEARS all the way home in a taxi, but she cheered up when they arrived at her house and Jeff ordered, "Start cooking, Gram. Get the biggest steak you can buy, because I'm still hungry enough to eat a horse!"

He heard her happily ordering groceries over the telephone. His first thought was to look in the bushes. Sure enough, there were the bags, sodden from the rain.

He felt restless. He was uneasy about Sarge and anxious to get him back. He busied himself emptying the suitcases and hanging his and Trudy's things to dry on the clothesline.

Word had gotten around, and the neighbors started dropping in. Soon Jeff had quite an audience. The ladies went in the house to help Gram get ready for company, but the children and fathers

116

listened and asked questions. The men were really upset that none of them had noticed that Gram's blue boat was missing.

It was still missing, as far as anybody knew.

Finally Jeff and Gram were left alone. She offered him bananas, but he shuddered, remembering how awful a banana could get when it dissolved. He made himself a peanut butter and bacon sandwich. He was still restless, roaming the house, watching for his parents, waiting for the police to bring Sarge.

He made up a big dish of food, and Gram contributed some very fine tidbits she knew Sarge would like. Jeff perched on a kitchen stool, keeping her company. She was busy preparing a real feast, but she kept glancing at him. "Jeff, you've changed," she said.

"Sure. I never was this hungry before."

"You're thinner, of course, and you seem older, but that's not exactly it. You're — well, I've always thought you were a nice boy."

"What you mean is, I was a brat," Jeff said, grinning. He and Gram had always been good friends.

She was too shaken by the events of the day to joke with him. "You and Trudy have changed," she said. "Toward each other, I mean."

Jeff didn't answer. If there was one thing he dreaded, it was that Trudy would tell a lot of mushy things about him — how he had changed and how she thought he was nicer and all that. He dreaded to have his family talking about him.

The wail of a siren brought him to the front door. It also brought all the kids in the neighborhood on the run. A police car stopped at the curb.

Officer Kelly tried to hold him, but Sarge broke free when he saw Jeff. The policeman looked somewhat the worse for wear. However, he didn't look as though he had been bitten, which was what Jeff had been fearing all day. Sarge reared up on his hind legs and put his paws on Jeff's shoulders, and Jeff staggered under his weight. The dog slobbered with joy, expressing his relief that they were together again.

The children fought to get to Sarge, wanting to pet him. Sarge was kind of a hero too. Jeff got a firm grip on his collar. "I have to feed him," he told them. "Come back to see him after supper."

Gram was fond of Sarge, although she often complained about his enormous appetite. She was at the door to meet him, but Jeff led him straight to the kitchen. He handed him the plate of food, and Sarge wolfed it down. He gave him a bowl of water and he lapped it all, throwing a shower of drops around Gram's kitchen.

Then and only then did Jeff dare let go of the leash. Gram sat down and Sarge put his head in her lap, and she cradled his rough head in her hands, talking to him lovingly. When she looked up her eyes were brimming with tears, and she told Officer Kelly, "Everything makes me cry today, but I never expected to blubber over a big useless beast like this one!"

"Did he give you a bad time?" Jeff asked the policeman.

"Yes, he did. He's the first dog I ever met I couldn't make friends with. We had quite a struggle getting him into the boat. But I didn't blame him. He's had a tough experience, and losing you was the last straw. I thought we might have to take him to a vet until we were sure he's safe, but he's obviously all right. We'll go along now. Goodbye, ma'am. Take care of yourself, Jeff."

"Thanks for everything," Jeff called after him.

"He's a nice man," Gram said.

"He sure is," Jeff told her.

Jeff wandered into the living room, Sarge at his heels. He stood at the window, waiting for the newspaper, waiting for his parents. He felt very

119

queer. It was a comfort to have Sarge's hard body pressed against him.

He saw the paper boy turn the corner. Some of the neighborhood kids were still waiting outside. They took the paper and knocked on the door. "You're right on the front page, Jeff," they told him. He thanked them and managed to shut the door.

"Gram," he called. She came in, wiping her hands on her apron. They sat on the sofa and read the story together. Yes, there on the front page was a picture of Trudy in a hospital bed, Jeff standing beside her. Below was another of Middle Hump, taken from an airplane. The island looked tiny.

"CHILDREN RESCUED, LOST SINCE TUESDAY," the headline read. The story went on:

This morning at 10 A.M. a helicopter belonging to the Bridgeton Police Department rescued two persons from Middle Hump, one of the islands lying across the entrance to Bridgeton Harbor. The story which was revealed is so bizarre as to be almost unbelievable.

Earlier in the morning the Department had received a call from Mr. E. M. Tobias, of New York City. Mr. Tobias, the owner of a small private plane, reported that while making an emergency landing yesterday at Bridgeton Airport, he had flown over the harbor and thought he might have seen an SOS on one of the islands. The sky was so overcast he was not sure his observation was correct. His doubt, he said, preyed on his mind and he decided to inform the authorities this morning.

Some time later, when the fog began to lift, the Department's helicopter took to the air. The pilot, Officer George Olson, and his companion, Officer Henry Kelly, spotted a large SOS marked in the sand on the north shore of Middle Hump. When they landed they were met by two children, Jeffrey Pennell, aged 12, and his sister Gertrude, 9, of New Millbrook. The story the children told, which they later repeated for this reporter, confirms that they had been living alone on the island, with little food or water, since Tuesday last.

According to Jeffrey, they arrived on that day at the home of their grandmother, Mrs. James Pennell of 37 Greenwood Street, West Bridgeton. Mrs. Pennell was expecting the children later in the week. She was not at home on Tuesday afternoon, and Jeff and Trudy were anxious to go for a swim. They took some food, and with their dog, a German shepherd named Sarge, they set out in a rowboat.

They reached Middle Hump and were enjoying their swim when they discovered that the tide had come in and carried off their boat. Jeff attempted to rescue it but was unsuccessful. They had brought ashore their few supplies, a Thermos bottle of milk and a bag of cookies and bananas. Finding themselves marooned, the children set out to survive, expecting however to be rescued soon.

The account of their days on the sandy, treeless island is a story of ingenuity and courage. Although each attempts to give all the credit to the other, it is clear that both are unusually intelligent and resourceful young people. They made their headquarters in an abandoned shack. By rationing their food they warded off extreme hunger, despite the fact that they shared what they had with Sarge, their dog.

Both became badly sunburned. Thursday's rain provided them with fresh water, which they desperately needed. They also managed to open two cans of tomato juice which they found in the shack. The cold and dampness of their barren island resulted in the little girl suffering a bad cold. Despite this and the nightmare of their abandonment on the island they were in remarkably good spirits when rescued.

The helicopter brought the pair to the airport, where an ambulance carried them to the hospital. Jeffrey showed no ill effects from his experience, but his sister is being kept for a few days, for treatment and observation.

One obvious lesson may be drawn from this episode. It points up the danger of allowing children the casual use of boats on the harbor, without adequate supervision by adults.

The question still remains how two children could find themselves in such a desperate plight within sight of a busy city. When this reporter questioned Mr. John Hofstadt, Commissioner of Police, Mr. Hofstadt answered that his police budget does not provide for personnel to maintain a regular patrol of the harbor. The police boat and helicopter are kept on a standby basis, for use when needed.

The Pennell children make it clear they blame only themselves for their adventure. Their story, cheerfully told, made something else clear to this reporter, who interviewed them at the Bridgeton Hospital. The worriers who fear that the younger generation is soft and helpless should take heart. Trudy and Jeff Pennell, deprived of the comforts and necessities of civilization for several days, survived very well.

That was the end. "Hey," Jeff blurted, "we're famous!"

"You are," Gram said heartily, "you're truly famous and I'm so proud of you I could bust, and so will your folks be. Now I've got to get back to my cooking. Come and keep me company."

"I'll be right along," he said.

He didn't hurry. He wanted to read the story again, slowly. There was so much that couldn't go in, so much he and Trudy hadn't told and might never tell. He wondered if Trudy had a copy of the paper at the hospital.

The telephone rang. "It's your dad, and he wants you," Gram called.

"Jeff?" Mr. Pennell's voice sounded strained. "Your mother and I just got to Bridgeton, and we're going to the hospital first to see your sister. Then we'll come straight out to Gram's. We can hardly wait to see you. Thank God you're all right!"

"Okay, Dad. We'll see you soon."

"You are all right, aren't you, son?"

"Sure, I'm great. I'll see you, Dad."

The sound of his father's voice made Jeff feel suddenly very blue. He knelt down and hugged Sarge. The big dog opened one eye and thumped his tail, then went back to sleep. The loneliness that had always haunted Jeff was back with him now. He had forgotten for a few days how alone he usually felt when he was with his family.

Gram was humming while she rattled pans. Jeff thought, "Everybody else gets along with other people. Why can't I? Dad and Mom want to see me, sure, but they have to see Trudy first. She comes first; like she always did and always will."

He ranged the house, looking out of windows, waiting. His better sense said, "That's stupid.

Mother and Dad went to the hospital because Trudy's the sick one. So why do you want to make a federal case of a little thing like that?"

Then the weirdest thought intruded. He caught himself wishing he was back on the island. That *was* dumb! Why would anybody ever want to be on a stinking little island like Middle Hump?

Well, the answer was he had shared that miserable island with Trudy. When they had nobody but each other for comfort, he and his sister had begun to feel close to each other. Trudy had begun to trust and like him.

Was that going to be spoiled, now they were back in civilization? Would they act the way they used to, bickering and fighting all the time like enemies? Did he have to be the lone wolf again? Would he have to act ornery because Trudy was the pet of the family and he wanted some attention too?

He didn't want to. As a matter of fact, he wished he would never have to act mean and selfish again. But his own particular loneliness was back with him, and he didn't know how to cope with it.

Gram recalled him from his sour thoughts. "Jeff, I heard a car stop, didn't I? Look and see, will you?"

He peered out. Dusk had come along the quiet

street. "It's the folks," he called. His dad's cream-colored station wagon had pulled up. Mom was getting out, and she had her arm around Trudy.

The three came up the walk. Jeff opened the door. His mother folded him in her arms, clinging to him as though she could never let him go, calling him "my dearest boy, my darling son." Then his father got hold of him and hugged him until Jeff's ribs hurt. Sarge circled around them, whining happily.

Jeff was really shaken. There was such tender love in his mother's face. Also, it was years since he had hugged his dad. He had figured that was sissy stuff and his father would hate it.

"Hey, isn't anybody interested that *I'm* here?" Trudy chirped.

She patted Jeff's arm, trying to tell him something. Tell him what?

"How did you get out of the hospital?" he asked her.

"I wasn't really sick, so they had to let me go. I talked my way out of that place. Did you see the paper?"

"I saw it."

"We're very, very proud of our two children," their mother said, smiling, her eyes brimming.

"We want to hear the whole story from you," Mr. Pennell added.

Trudy and Jeff were silent, and he guessed she was thinking the same thing he was. They wouldn't be able in a million years to tell the story the way it really was. That was something that belonged just to them. As long as they lived, even when they got to be old, their days on Middle Hump would be a piece of time they could share only with each other.

"Come help me get the dinner on, Molly," Gram called to their mother.

Mr. Pennell was contending with Sarge, who was beside himself with joy to have his whole family together again.

Jeff and Trudy were left alone. "Hey, those pictures were pretty good," Jeff said.

"Yes. At least we didn't look so filthy dirty. Not that I looked like any glamour-puss or anything." Trudy fell silent.

She acted uneasy, picking at the bandages on her arms. "What's the matter with you, peanuts?" Jeff asked.

"Do you know why I talked my way out of that hospital?" Trudy burst out. Her face was red with embarrassment. "Oh, it was all right; the nurses were great and all that. But I got lonesome. *You* weren't there."

Suddenly Jeff's heart felt as light as a balloon. Happiness flooded through him. "Don't tell me you missed me," he scoffed. "After the time we had? You missed me like a hole in the head!"

"I got lonesome for your ugly face and your horrible disposition," Trudy said, scowling. "Everybody was too nice. I'm more used to having somebody yelling at me!"

Their mother was at the door. "Children, dinner's ready." Then she looked hurt and puzzled, for she saw the scowl on Trudy's face. "You children aren't fighting with each other, are you?" she asked. "I thought — "

"Sure, we're fighting," Jeff said, and gave Trudy a loving bang on the back that almost knocked her down. She countered with a slap at his face.

He caught Trudy's hand. "If we want to fight, we will, won't we, nitwit?" he barked at his sister. "I don't know who's got a better right!"